· THE ·
HANDBUILT
Home

34 Simple, Stylish & Budget-Friendly
Woodworking Projects for Every Room

ANA WHITE

POTTER
CRAFT

New York

For my readers, thank you for everything. And for Jacob, Grace, and my family, thank you for believing in me.

Copyright © 2012 by Ana White

All rights reserved.
Published in the United States by Potter Craft,
an imprint of the Crown Publishing Group,
a division of Random House, Inc., New York.
www.pottercraft.com
www.crownpublishing.com

POTTER CRAFT and colophon are registered trademarks of Random House, Inc.

Some of the material in this work was previously published on www.ana-white.com.

Library of Congress Control Number: 2012936933

ISBN 978-0-307-58732-9
eISBN 978-0-307-58733-6

Printed in China

Design by Laura Palese

Photographs by Ana White, unless otherwise noted:
page 2: Ashley Mills, Crystal Rose; page 4: Kristen Duke;
page 7: Amanda Crawford; pages 9-14 Amanda Clark;
page 16: Charity Fielder; page 17: PureBond Plywood;
pages 19-22: Amanda Clark; page 23: (top) Crystal Rose;
page 30: (bottom left) Ashley Mills; page 41: Ashley Mills;
pages 46-47: (left) Jaime Costiglio, (bottom left) Whitney
Gainer, (top) Ana White, (bottom right) Hillary Dickman;
page 49: Jaime Costiglio; page 56-61: Hillary Dickman;
page 65: Whitney Gainer; page 68-69: (left, bottom left)
Ashley Mills, (top, bottom right) Rebecca Ridner; pages
72-79: Rebecca Ridner; pages 83: Ashley Mills; page 85:
(right) Ashley Turner, (bottom right) Crystal Rose; page
97: Ashley Turner; page 100: Crystal Rose; pages 104-
105: (far left, far right) Amanda Clark, (bottom left) Layla
Palmer, (top, bottom right)Brook Wilhelmsen; pages 107-
109: Brook Wilhelmsen; pages110-113: Amanda Clark;
page 115: Cherish Fielder; page 119: Brook Wilhelmsen;
page 120: Layla Palmer; page 131: Amanda Crawford;
pages 134-135 (top, bottom) Amanda Clark, (bottom
right) Shaunna and Matt West; page 140: Amanda Clark;
page 146 Shaunna and Matt West; page 148: Amanda
Clark; pages 154-155: (bottom left) Amy Huntley, (top)
Kirsten Wright, (bottom right) Rebecca Ridner; pages
157, 161: Amy Huntley; pages 163,167: Kirsten Wright;
page 168: Rebecca Ridner; pages 172-173: (top) Lydia
Manders

Front cover photographs (from top): Kristen Duke,
Rebecca Ridner, Amanda Clark, Crystal Rose, and
Ashley Mills

10 9 8 7 6 5

First Edition

CONTENTS

INTRODUCTION

Do you ever look at furniture and think, "I could build that"? Guess what? You absolutely can.

Just a decade ago, I would look at furniture and wish I could build it, but at the time I lacked the ability and skills, and I couldn't find any information to help me learn how to make the type of furniture I wanted.

Now, I'm a do-it-yourself furniture maker, mother, homemaker, and lover of pretty hardware, pink paint, and white drawer slides. Now, I look at furniture, and say, "I can build that," and then I go straight to my garage and make it.

From beds to coffee tables, chairs to wood toys, even kitchens and playhouses—you name it, I've built it.

I've created hundreds of pieces of furniture, designed thousands of furniture plans, and enjoyed knowing that people all over have made many projects using my ideas.

But initially, though I was obsessed with furniture, though I had learned to hunt down discarded items to refinish, I had never built a piece from scratch.

When I found out I was pregnant with my daughter, my husband and I were living in our garage, saving to build a home. Knowing a baby was on the way, I drew up a house plan on graph paper, and we started building. We could not afford contractors, so board by board, we built our own home by hand. My husband would say, "I'll hold the board, and you nail," and I would close my eyes, hold my breath, and squeeze the nail-gun trigger.

And guess what? I discovered that when done properly, using power tools was not a matter of strength or courage, but rather a matter of a little know-how and experience. Soon I was using saws, drills, and routers, and eventually my husband even gave me the greatest present ever: my very own tape measure.

Unfortunately, my daughter learned to crawl on the garage floor because there is only so much one family with a newborn baby, building paycheck to paycheck, can get done in a short Alaska summer. But ultimately, we built our home and saved hundreds of thousands of dollars in the process.

And something else was built: my confidence and knowledge as a builder.

When we moved into our new home we had no money for furniture. For a year, we slept on a mattress on the floor, keeping our clothing in baskets piled in the corner. I refused to buy low-quality particleboard furniture to get us by, but I could not afford the high-quality contemporary pieces I appreciated and loved.

And then one day, I decided that if we could build a house, I should try my hand at furniture.

I drew a plan for a bed on scratch paper. This bed would be built from off-the-shelf materials, the most basic of tools—just a drill and a saw—and was simple and easy enough for me to work on in the precious little time my infant daughter was sleeping. I used leftover boards from our house, bought eighty dollars in new supplies, including paint and hardware, and I built our farmhouse bed (page 136). We sleep on this very same bed, so many years later, and it still is as sturdy, strong, and beautiful as ever.

In the years that followed, I became obsessed with building furniture. I made bookcases, cabinets, and even sofas. Yet I stayed true to the principles of my original farmhouse bed—keeping plans simple, using standard off-the-shelf materials, and working with the most basic tools, but making up for these limitations with a well-thought-out design. Even today, hundreds of projects later, I still build with the same easy-to-buy materials.

Building furniture has brought me great joy and happiness. It has both given me confidence and humbled me. Our entire family has spent countless hours in the garage, working on project after project, yet I never tire of taking simple boards and basic materials and turning them into an attractive, usable piece of furniture. I still get tingles and can't sleep at night when I am in the middle of a project, and I often find myself amazed over what can be accomplished with a few pieces of wood.

But the greatest joy of all for me is sharing my passion with others. Each time I help someone build a picnic table or a bench, or even just a simple picture frame, it's as if I rediscover the pleasure of learning how to build all over again.

This book is for non-woodworkers, people like me years ago, who want to make their own attractive, modern furniture but just haven't yet found the confidence or the skills to do so. You don't need to be physically tough or superstrong to learn to use a power tool, and it is okay if you don't know that a 2x4 doesn't actually measure 2" x 4"; all you need is determination to make a better home for yourself or your family. I've been there. I know it's not easy to squeeze a nail-gun trigger for the first time, or even to load a drill bit when you don't know how. But I can tell you this—if I can do it, so can you. And I've written this book specifically to help you.

This book will cover everything you need to know to begin building your own furniture, from the basic tools you will require and how to use them to selecting boards to actually building and finishing your projects—a beginner can become a builder with confidence. There are starter projects that I suggest you tackle first to gain some experience.

For those of you with more building experience, this book includes thirty-four of my best plans—a few are some of the all-time favorites from my blog, but most are totally new—that you can jump right to and start building. I've included several advanced projects to keep you challenged, but I know even the starter projects can be useful when decorating your home or making a gift.

Regardless of your skill, your budget, how much time you have, or even what tools you own, you can build amazing furniture and save thousands of dollars off retail.

Today is your day to say, "I can build that."

· ICON KEY ·

Each project includes icons that will tell you the skill level, cost, and time necessary for completion.

Starter	Beginner	Intermediate	Advanced

$	$$	$$$
less than $50	less than $100	more than $100

½	1	2
Afternoon	Day	Weekend

10 REASONS TO DIY

There are good reasons why tens of thousands of other people, many of them women, are taking up DIY furniture.

1 **DIY IS WALLET FRIENDLY.**
Building furniture is the best craft or hobby for saving money. If you make your own cards, you might save a few dollars. If you make your own curtains, you might save a hundred dollars. But if you furnish your home with hand-built furniture, you could be saving thousands of dollars.

2 **IT'S CUSTOM-MADE FOR YOU.**
Would a hot pink nightstand make your room? Or do you have an oddly shaped mudroom that you can't find the right storage cabinet for? If you build your own furniture, you are in complete control and can easily customize your project to suit your specific needs.

3 **IT MAKES YOUR HOME HEALTHIER.**
In today's homes, we are increasingly aware of indoor air quality. We install air purifiers and paint walls with low volatile organic compound (VOC) paints. But did you know your furniture could be making your air quality less healthy?

Recently listed by the government as a known cancer-causing agent, formaldehyde is found in most pressed-wood furniture. And most furniture does not list the type of chemical finishes applied. If you build your own furniture, you can choose what materials you put into your home and use nontoxic varnishes and polishes, improving the air quality and, ultimately, the health of your family.

4 **IT KEEPS YOU FIT.**
Did you know building furniture burns upward of three hundred calories per hour? You could skip the gym and put all that time and energy into producing amazing furniture. Carpentry and furniture building is a total-body workout. You will use muscles you did not know you have. Having a physically intensive hobby is a fun and healthy way of staying in shape with minimal effort.

5 IT UPGRADES YOUR FURNITURE.

Nothing is more frustrating than to finally find that perfect end table, just to discover the legs are easily dented, or to fill a designer bookcase, only to notice the shelf sagging soon after. Rather than become saddened that your armoire is backed with cardboard, you can make your own furniture as high quality as you want. You can reinforce shelves, add extra screws, or put on a real plywood back. Your project is yours to make as high quality as you need it to be.

6 IT IS ECOFRIENDLY.

When you buy furniture from a retail store, it most likely has taken a long journey before you purchased it. First lumber is milled and shipped thousands of miles to factories, where it is turned into furniture. Then the furniture is wrapped in a ton of packaging and shipped thousands of miles back to distribution centers. From there it's shipped to retailers and ultimately sold to consumers. Packaging waste, fuel usage and exhaust, and unnecessary extra steps are all taxing on our environment.

When you build your own furniture, you can choose locally grown, fast-renewing wood species. You can use reclaimed or discarded wood. And you will be avoiding extra packing and shipping. Building your own furniture is generally greener than purchasing it.

7 IT MAKES A MEANINGFUL HANDMADE GIFT.

There is just something about a handmade gift that is priceless, perhaps because it means someone cared enough to dedicate their time to making something by hand. Perhaps it is knowing that you are special enough to have something no one else does. Or maybe it is just a perfect fit, something you could never buy. My favorite projects are those that I gift. I find I can stretch my gift-giving budget so much farther by adding my time and creativity.

8 DIY IS EMPOWERING.

It is life changing to be able to turn 2x4s into home furnishings. I have found myself more confident to tackle all sorts of other projects, from fixing the washing machine to hanging curtains. This confidence has spread throughout my life, giving me an "I can do that!" attitude that makes me more positive and adventurous.

9 IT'S REWARDING.

Most of us live lives of maintenance. Cleaning, doing laundry, going to work, paying bills, making dinner—these are daily tasks that offer little to improve our lifestyles, and on a daily basis, it is hard to see progress. The majority of our time is spent on long lists of "musts" rather than on activities that feed our spirit.

Building is a positive experience that is rewarding to your heart, soul, brain, and budget. Mastering new skills and turning raw materials into something functional engages your mind and creativity, gives you a personal connection to items you use every day, and offers an enormous sense of accomplishment.

10 IT IS FUN!

I find myself getting out of bed earlier to go work on a project, sneaking off during my daughter's nap time to do some sanding, begging for five extra minutes of time to finish painting. In our adult life, how often can you do something that is truly fun? I encourage you to give furniture building a try—I know you will love it as much as I do!

·1·
GETTING STARTED

You are going to make beautiful furniture. Gorgeous, sturdy, one-of-a-kind, handmade furniture.

People are going to say, "You? *You* made your own furniture?"

And you are going to proudly reply, "Yes, I did it all myself."

But before we get to the building part, we must cover the basics. This book is not just about building furniture. It is about building furniture smartly and safely.

tools and equipment

Just as you need a sewing machine to sew or a mixer to bake, you will need some tools to build your own furniture. But unlike traditional carpentry books, the tools you will need to build the furniture in this book are fairly basic, and most serve a variety of purposes. You may find you already own many of them.

BUYING TOOLS

If you are just starting out and do not have all the tools listed here, do not be discouraged. One of the most inspiring e-mails I have ever received was from a reader who built projects by asking her home improvement store to make the board cuts and then assembling and fastening her pieces with simple

hammer and nails. Her projects were beautiful. Determination can be your most valuable tool.

There are quite a few projects in this book that you can make with just a drill, hammer, and nails. My advice is to borrow tools or use tools you already own for the first few projects you attempt. I know you are going to love furniture building, but I want you to invest in high-quality tools, so try a few projects to get a better idea of what you like before going tool shopping.

Save up and buy the best possible tools you can afford. These tools are an investment, and what you make with them can potentially save you thousands of dollars in home furnishings, gifts, and other home improvement or DIY tasks. These tools will pay for themselves, sometimes even in just a single project.

TYPES OF TOOLS

In this book, I've broken down tools into four categories: basic tools, cutting tools, fastening tools, and finishing tools. Basic tools are items such as tape measures and levels that you will use throughout the entire building process; you will want to keep them on hand while purchasing boards through setting up the finished project in your home. Cutting tools are used to cut boards or other materials. Fastening tools are used to assemble your boards into furniture. And finishing tools are used to smooth, paint, and complete the transformation of your woodworking projects into beautiful furniture.

WRENCH

HAMMER

CARPENTER PENCIL

SCREWDRIVER

ADJUSTABLE PLIERS

TAPE MEASURE

L-SQUARE RULER

NEEDLE-NOSE PLIERS

SPEED SQUARE

HAND SAW

CLAMPS

TAPE MEASURE   **SPEED SQUARE**

basic tools

You probably already own many of these basic tools. These are the tools you will find yourself using throughout the building process—and throughout many other home improvement projects. Keep basic tools readily available, as you will need them for most projects. I like to store my basic tools in a wooden toolbox, next to my work surface.

TAPE MEASURE Your tape measure is going to become your best friend and will be the most-used tool in building furniture. You will use your tape measure countless times, so it is important that you choose one that fits in your hand and is easy for you to use and to read. Tape measures come in a variety of sizes; for the projects in this book, a 12-foot (3.7m) tape measure is fine.

Each tape measure is different, but most standard tape measures have a moving end hook, to accommodate both pulled and pushed measurements. Check the instructions that come with your tape measure, or take a minute to measure a board both by pulling (taking an outside measurement by placing the hook over one end and pulling to extend the tape) and pushing (taking an inside measurement by extending the tape and adding the length of the case to ensure the two match.

SPEED SQUARE A speed square or carpenter's square is an L-shaped tool with edges in a perfect 90-degree angle. The square will help you quickly mark boards for cuts and mark board joints before joining them. It is also used to check joints made at 90-degree angles for accuracy or square, to check corners for square, and to mark angles, and it can be used for quick,

short measurements. This inexpensive tool is a must for building straight and square projects. Buy a 12" (30.5cm) speed square to begin, and add a 6" (15cm) speed square for tighter spots and smaller boards.

CLAMPS Clamps are more than an extra hand—they do jobs that you will not. Clamping boards during the project steps ensures that the boards stay put while you work on them. Use clamps to hold boards down while you cut, to hold boards in a tight spot while you nail, and to hold joints together overnight while glue dries. Invest in at least two clamps and keep them near your work surface. Keeping tools accessible puts me in the habit of using them on every step.

HAMMER This book rarely specifically calls for the use of a hammer, but having a hammer within reach is necessary for building projects. You will use it to place boards in tight spots, remove wayward nails, or attach trim if you don't have a nailer.

Choose a small hammer with a smooth head to avoid damaging your project. Avoid tapping directly on the raw wood of your project with the hammer. Instead, use a scrap piece of wood in between the project and your hammer to protect the finished project from dents.

PENCIL You will need something to mark your cuts and joints. I prefer mechanical pencils, but many woodworkers use carpenter's pencils, which are flat so they won't roll. Use whatever works for you. I often keep three pencils handy—one on my work surface, one at my saw, and one behind my ear. Anything you can do to minimize searching for tools or making additional trips between your work zone and your cutting zone saves time and energy.

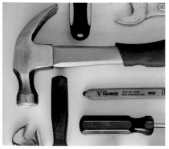

CLAMPS   **HAMMER**

CHALK LINE A chalk line is a roll of string coated in chalk, inside a container. The string is pulled out one end of the chalk line and then retracted by winding back up. The chalk-coated string is pulled tight between two measured points, and the center of the chalked string is snapped to leave a straight line between the two points. Chalk lines are especially useful when marking straight lines for long cuts on plywood and, when done properly, will create a straight line.

NEEDLE-NOSE PLIERS Like the screwdrivers and the hammer, in this book you will rarely see specific references to needle-nose pliers. Because if all goes perfectly, you won't need them. But as an experienced DIYer, I guarantee that nails sometimes do not do what you want. Having a pair of needle-nose pliers on hand will help you remove rogue nails. Simply grab the protruding nail tip at the end, and bend back and forth until the nail comes free.

cutting tools

Having the right cutting tools for the project can simplify the process and help you build better projects. A nice clean cut makes for a nice clean joint.

When you are cutting, always factor in the width of the saw blade. Unlike cutting with scissors, cutting wood creates sawdust, resulting in lost material at the cut. Depending on your saw blade, this can be anywhere from ⅛" to ¼" lost at each cut. It is best to measure, cut, then measure again, as opposed to marking out all of your cuts and cutting because of the saw blade width factor.

JIGSAW A jigsaw is used for making curved or arched cuts, and for finishing cuts made with a round or circular saw. You can use a jigsaw to make straight cuts (and many people do), but they are not as precise as cuts made with a circular saw blade.

Of all the saws, the jigsaw tends to be the least intimidating and least expensive saw, and many people make a jigsaw their first saw purchase. Jigsaws are a good starting point for the beginning woodworker.

When you cut with a jigsaw, you need to support the entire board you are cutting and leave clearance under the board for the jigsaw blade. Understand that

JIGSAW   CIRCULAR SAW

a jigsaw blade is very flimsy, so when cutting arches or shapes in thicker wood, the jigsaw blade may angle or curve, even if the cut appears perfect at the surface.

Most jigsaws can be adjusted to cut at angles and to different depths. Take time to understand all of the features of your jigsaw and practice using it.

CIRCULAR SAW With a circular saw you can build most any project in this book. Circular saws are also relatively affordable. Most are highly adjustable, allowing you to cut beveled edges and even adjust the depth of your cuts.

But circular saws can be difficult to use and require extra steps to make cuts, including marking cuts, supporting boards, and clamping boards in place. They also require practice and experience before a user can consistently make straight, square cuts.

COMPOUND MITER SAW A compound miter saw (also referred to as a chop saw, radial arm saw, or miter saw) is a saw that is held fixed on a stand while the board being cut is fully supported on both ends. To make a cut, simply place the board on the saw, pushed firmly against the fence (a straight guide at the back of the saw), and pull the saw down. As long as your board is held square to the fence, the saw will cut square. If your compound miter saw cuts bevels and angles, you can make these cuts quickly and easily by adjusting the saw.

For me, having a compound miter saw was like having a serger (or overlock sewing machine) to create seams. My compound miter saw helps me make straight square cuts with accuracy, precision, and speed each time. But a compound miter saw is more expensive than other saws. I recommend buying the most expensive compound miter saw you can afford.

If you can get a sliding compound miter saw, a feature that allows you to cut wider width boards with the same ease, save for it. You will not regret any of its added features and options.

TABLE SAW Very few of the plans in this book will require the use of a table saw. However, as you become more experienced in building furniture, you may wish to invest in one. The primary use for a table saw is to rip boards (cut boards in long cuts with the wood grain) down to a specific width. For example, you may need to rip plywood into 16"- (40.5cm-) wide strips. With a table saw, you simply set the fence, a simple guide on the table saw, at 16" (40.5cm) and run the plywood through the table saw, achieving an even cut, rip after rip.

The plans in this book use standard off-the-shelf lumber dimensions. Sometimes lumber is not true to width, and you may wish to rip the lumber down to true width.

But a circular saw can do all of these tasks. And most home improvement stores will rip plywood for you. The table saw is a nice-to-have-but-not-necessary tool for the beginning furniture builder.

fastening tools

Once your boards are all cut, you will need a means to fasten the boards together to create your furniture. Similar to how most retail furniture is made today, I recommend pocket hole joints created quickly and

SCREWDRIVERS

DRILL

easily with a simple pocket hole jig for joining boards into furniture.

Some projects can be simply glued and nailed together, especially those with a full face frame, or trim boards on the front to further enhance joints. Many projects can also be put together with trim screws and a countersinking drill bit to hide screw heads beneath the surface of your project. Each project provides different means to assemble it, with pocket holes typically creating the strongest joint, countersinking screws being less strong and requiring more work to conceal, and nails making the weakest but easiest joint.

SCREWDRIVERS You probably already have a set of screwdrivers around the house. You will want to keep screwdrivers handy as you build. From tightening up a screwed joint to fixing a tool or changing a saw blade, attaching hardware, and even distressing a finish, make sure you have at least a Phillips-head and a flat-head screwdriver in your apron or toolbox

DRILL Your drill is one of your most important tools. You'll use it for everything from drilling pocket holes and pilot holes—holes drilled to ease driving screws and prevent wood splitting—to driving screws. Choose a drill that fits comfortably in your hand and is easy for you to use. A cordless drill is a luxury worth splurging on, but make sure the cordless drill has enough power to drill pocket holes and drive long screws.

DRILL BITS With your drill, you will need drill bits. A basic starter set will include all of the essentials, or you can buy drill bits to match your screw heads. Drill bits are used for everything from drilling pilot holes for attaching hardware to driving screws into material.

SAW SAFETY

• Always use the right saw for the application—using a saw incorrectly is an opportunity for an accident.

• When using a saw, never stand directly in front of or behind the board you are cutting. The force of the saw could push the board unexpectedly forward or backward, resulting in injury.

• Always read the instructions on your saw and have a good understanding of your saw's safety features and the proper use of the saw.

• Never make a cut if you are not comfortable. To increase your comfort, use clamps to hold boards down.

• Support both ends of each cut so that the board does not pinch the saw blade as you are cutting. This can result in the unsupported board twisting or flipping.

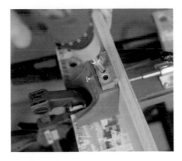

POCKET HOLE JIG

LEVEL

FINISH NAILER Think of this as a staple gun that can tack wood together with speed and ease. Although it's entirely possible to hand nail trim onto a surface, a finish nailer will reduce the amount of time and complexity in building furniture. Finish nailers are also designed to drive a nail just below the surface of the wood, making the hole easy to hide.

Finish nailers come in a variety of sizes. I find the 18-gauge finish nailer to be the most versatile, because it shoots nails from ⅝" (16mm) long to 2" (5cm) long—covering the range of nail sizes needed to build all of the projects in this book.

The best use for finish nailers is securing trim to your project or face frames. But I know many well-respected carpenters who use finish nailers as the primary fastening tool to construct wall systems and built-ins. Just don't forget the glue when using nails—glue bonds the woods together, creating a joint stronger than the nails themselves will.

POCKET HOLE JIG A pocket hole jig is a simple tool that guides you in drilling holes at an angle and driving screws through this predrilled hole to create strong, precise joints quickly and easily. Most furniture produced today uses pocket hole joinery because of its strength and precision.

For many years I successfully built projects without a pocket hole jig, and so can you. But I highly recommend the pocket hole jig, because it will enable you to build stronger projects more easily. Your joints will be more precise, you will have more control while joining boards, and the joint is stronger than attaching to the end grain.

The pocket hole jig also solves a large problem: It enables you to join boards together edge to edge.

With a pocket hole jig, you can build door frames and tabletops without adding extra blocking underneath, saving you materials and time. This will pay for itself by allowing you to build projects that last longer.

COUNTERSINK BIT A countersink bit is a drill bit that simultaneously drills a pilot hole and a screw head pocket hole. The pilot hole is simply a hole drilled in the wood to match the screw shafts to prevent the wood from splitting. The screw head pocket hole is an indentation at the surface of the pilot hole to allow the screw head to sink below the surface of the wood. These bits are designed to predrill holes for fastening projects together with screws, sinking the screw heads below the surface of the project, which will be filled and finished later.

My favorite countersink bit is a quick change to a drill bit, with one end having a countersink bit and the other a drill bit. With a quick change drill bit, you can drill a countersink hole, flip the bit around, and drive the screw, saving you time and effort

TIP When countersinking, be careful to keep your drill straight and perpendicular to the board; countersinking bits are easy to break off, and broken bits can get expensive fast. Good news is most countersink bits are repairable, and the pilot hole bits are inexpensive.

LEVEL A level will help you make sure your project is straight. Though often measurements can be used to guide you when attaching boards, sometimes you need to check and make sure your project is level. For example, when adding a shelf to a project, not only should you measure the location of the joint but also check to make sure the shelf is level with a level. A level is also used to hang shelves straight on the wall. My go-to level for building furniture is 12" (30.5cm) long.

NAIL PUNCH If you are nailing your projects with a hammer, you will need a nail punch to push nail heads below the surface of the wood. Nail punches are inexpensive and should be purchased to match the size or your nail heads.

finishing tools

While every step of building is important, the finish tends to have the greatest visual impact on your project. Choosing the right tools is the ticket to achieving beautifully finished furniture.

PUTTY KNIFE A simple putty knife enables you to apply putty to imperfections and fastening holes with ease and wipe excess off cleanly. Putty knives are inexpensive, but they will save you hours of topping off wood filler or sanding overfilled holes.

SANDPAPER AND SANDING BLOCK Before applying a finish, you need to sand your project to smooth out any imperfections and create beautiful joints. Sanding will also remove excess wood filler applied over screw holes and other flaws, and prepare your wood to accept stain or primer and paint.

There are three basic grits of sandpaper that I keep on hand all the time: coarse, medium, and fine. A good rule of thumb is to start with the coarsest grain and work your way incrementally to fine as the finish progresses.

A sanding block is an inexpensive hand tool that holds sandpaper securely and allows you to apply pressure to the project you are sanding without any discomfort to your hand.

POWER SANDER Like a sanding block, the power sander will prepare your project for a finish, but the power sander takes the time and work out of sanding. A power sander can be corded or cordless. I use an orbital sander, or a power sander that works in an orbiting motion, for most of my projects.

PAINTBRUSH Use a good, high-quality paintbrush to ensure your projects receive a beautiful finish. Lower-quality brushes may start to lose strands in your finish and tend not to hold up as well over time. Fine-bristled brushes will leave fewer streaks and brush marks, and they apply paint more evenly. I prefer tapered 2½" (2.5cm) and 1½" (3.8cm) brushes. Use brushes for painting trim and for smaller areas and projects.

SANDPAPER

POWER SANDER

PAINT ROLLER For larger projects, instead of increasing the brush size, use a small paint roller. Cabinet roller kits can be purchased inexpensively and include a small roller, a small tray, and extra roller covers. Using a small roller will minimize paint waste and cleanup but maximize all the benefits of using rollers. Rollers provide even coverage, which is essential when painting large areas consistently and evenly.

PAINT SPRAYER Paint sprayers are expensive, require a paint booth or a ventilated area, use more paint, and are time-consuming to clean. Yet when painting a large project, or painting several projects the same color at the same time, a paint sprayer can ensure your projects receive a consistent and even finish.

There's no need to invest in a paint sprayer when starting out, but if you build large projects on a regular basis, or are building projects professionally, it may be a good idea to get one.

STAINING RAGS It's always a good idea to have a pile of rags on hand for cleanup on a project. I also use rags to apply and wipe off stain. Consider cutting up old T-shirts to use as staining rags.

GETTING COMFORTABLE

My first rule of safety when building is to ask, "Am I comfortable?"

Are you comfortable cutting with a saw, or are you apprehensive? Can you handle the nailer without holding your breath or closing your eyes? Are you working at the right height for you, or does your back ache afterward? Are you wearing adequate hearing protection when the saw is on? In my experience, if I am uncomfortable, I am more apt to get hurt.

As you go through the building process, take a moment to consider any discomfort you may have and take steps to minimize it, assessing whether you require additional equipment or need more practice with a particular tool.

tool safety

Be comfortable using tools before you start to build. Read the safety manuals for all of your tools, and ask for a demonstration the first time you use your power tools from someone with experience. Use clamps in place of your own hands—clamps free your hands and let you focus more completely on a task.

And never, ever do anything you are not comfortable doing. If you are apprehensive, spend some more time practicing and getting yourself familiar with your tools.

safety equipment

Wear ear and eye protection as you cut and drill, not only to save your senses, but to allow you to use your senses better as you work. You will be able to see and hear yourself think over the noise and dust particles created by a saw.

When cutting and sanding, it's also advisable to wear a dusk mask to protect yourself from inhaling sawdust. Some wood materials contain added chemicals that can be harmful to your health. It is no fun to build if you are coughing up sawdust or holding your breath!

work zone

Having an organized workspace that is easy to clean, with good storage for materials and tools, is essential. Creating dedicated stations for each task will save you time and frustration.

You may not have a large enough space for dedicated work areas, but before you start to work on your project, I encourage you to consider creating different work zones for each step of the process. Even if the space is only temporary, this will make each stage of the building process much easier.

WORKBENCH

Your workbench could be as simple as two sawhorses with a piece of plywood on top, or a fancy professional one costing thousands of dollars—just find a good, flat, level surface that is a comfortable height to work from. I use an old, sturdy farmhouse table (page 73) I constructed years ago, because I'm not afraid of cutting or drilling into it. What you use is not as important as how you use it.

Your workbench should be larger than the size of your project. It should be standard tabletop height of 30" to 36" (76cm–91cm) counter height to reduce back strain. Take a second to check that the top is level by resting your level on it in all directions and areas.

Keep your workbench free of tools, materials, and debris. Tools should be placed within easy reach and in close proximity to the workbench, either on a shelf or cart, but clear of your work surface. My pocket hole jig is attached to the end of my workbench for a dedicated drilling area.

Your workbench can also be used as your finishing table; just remember to remove all debris and sawdust from the area prior to painting—you don't want sawdust adhering to your freshly painted project. A good practice is to keep a paint drop cloth slightly larger than your worktable surface on hand. Simply throw over your worktable when you are painting or staining.

materials

I love building furniture because I am always astonished at what can be made from humble boards. But getting started can be overwhelming and confusing for a beginner. Take comfort that with a little knowledge, and a few trips to the lumber aisle, you soon will be working with confidence and style.

WOOD

Wood really is the ultimate material to work with.

To me, wood is the ultimate gift from our earth, usable to give us shelter, to provide heat, even to print this book; yet it is renewable, and when living, it recycles the very air we breathe. In the form of lumber, wood is easy to work with, beautiful, and inexpensive, but it is full of depth and richness that no other material can match. It is forgiving, yet sturdy and smooth. There is good reason why most furniture is made from wood, as are all the projects in this book.

Yet understanding the different types of wood and selecting the perfect wood for your projects can be confusing to a beginner. And wood prices, qualities, and species can vary greatly depending on where you live, so carefully read through this section before heading to the hardware store.

boards

Boards as referenced in this book are solid wood boards, sold in dimensional sizes as shown in the table below.

BOARD	ACTUAL DIMENSIONAL SIZE
1x2	¾" x 1½" (2cm x 3.8cm)
1x3	¾" x 2½" (2cm x 6.5cm)
1x4	¾" x 3½" (2cm x 9cm)
1x6	¾" x 5½" (2cm x 14cm)
1x8	¾" x 7¼" (2cm x 18.5cm)
1x10	¾" x 9¼" (2cm x 23.5cm)
1x12	¾" x 11¼" (2cm x 28.5cm)
2x2	1½" x 1½" (3.8cm x 3.8cm)
2x3	1½" x 2½" (3.8cm x 6.5cm)
2x4	1½" x 3½" (3.8cm x 9cm)
2x6	1½" x 5½" (3.8cm x 14cm)
2x8	1½" x 7¼" (3.8cm x 18.5cm)
2x10	1½" x 9¼" (3.8cm x 23.5cm)
2x12	1½" x 11¼" (3.8cm x 28.5cm)

However, actual board dimensional sizes can vary from those listed in this table depending on factors including milling and board shrinkage—they can even differ from board to board bought in the same lot. When you select boards, take a tape measure with you and check the dimensions of each board you purchase to avoid problems later.

If your boards do differ in sizes from the table above, make adjustments in the project plan. The project plans in this book assume your board widths are true to this table.

Only purchase boards that have been dried and are free of moisture. Green or wet boards can dramatically shrink, twist, or warp when drying. A good practice is to bring your boards into your home or garage a few days before beginning your project to ensure the boards acclimate to your home before building.

Crooked boards make crooked projects or, at the very least, create frustration for the builder. To select straight boards, hold one end of the board up to your eye, looking down the length of the board, as if it were an arrow on a bow, and check for straightness. Rotate the board to check all four sides.

Also inspect the board for cupping (concave curve up or down), especially prevalent in wider boards. A board with cupping in it will create projects with uneven shelves or sides. Avoid these boards.

Imperfections such as cracks or splits on the surface of the wood should also be avoided. Knots can be concealed under paint, but they can cause boards to split or crack, or to warp to one side, so choose boards with smaller knots, and, if possible, try to cut the knots off when making cuts.

Store your boards flat, on a level surface, preferably still banded to other boards. Boards can warp or twist while being stored, so check your boards again before starting a project.

BIRCH	CHERRY	MAPLE
(HARDWOOD)	(HARDWOOD)	(HARDWOOD)
PINE	RED OAK	WALNUT
(SOFTWOOD)	(HARDWOOD)	(HARDWOOD)

Hardwood is a great choice for doors, drawer faces, and face frames because it holds up better than other wood choices. Softwood is very forgiving to work with. It is a great choice for distressed finishes.

sheet goods

As you can see, working with boards creates many problems, and those problems tend to get larger as your boards get wider. Thus, most furniture manufacturers use sheet goods—including plywood, MDF, and particleboard—for the bulk of the project and only trim the face of the project with solid wood boards.

Another limitation of boards is they do not come in standard widths wider than a 1x12 (or ¾" x 11¼" [2cm x 28.5cm]). For deeper storage projects, using sheet goods becomes a popular choice.

Sheet goods are sold in a variety of thicknesses and the following standard dimensions:

SHEET GOODS	SIZE
Full sheet of plywood	48" x 96" (122cm x 244cm)
½ sheet of plywood	48" x 48" (122cm x 122cm)
¼ sheet of plywood	48" x 24" (122cm x 61cm)
Full sheet of MDF	97" x 49" (246cm x 125cm)

A standard practice for all furniture that I design is to base the plans on standard board-width cuts, meaning that even if you choose to work with sheet goods, you still have the sheet goods ripped into board sizes that are more manageable and easier to work with. This way you are only making one cut per board, instead of having to cut shapes out of plywood, and your grains are all in the right direction. This practice not only simplifies building but saves you materials, allows you to have scraps that are reusable, and allows you to easily modify the depth of your projects. In most cases, you can simply swap out a 1x12 for a strip of plywood 16" (40.5cm) wide, or make the project narrower to fit your needs.

By taking a full sheet of ¾"- (2cm-) thick plywood and ripping it down into strips, you can create your own boards in any size up to 48" (122cm) wide. For example, instead of purchasing 1x12 boards, you could simply have your plywood ripped into strips 11¼" wide to create your own 1x12 boards from plywood. We tend to use 6" (15cm), 8" (20.5cm), 12" (30.5cm), 16" (40.5cm), and 24" (61cm) widths because these widths conserve

For beginners, I strongly recommend building with pine or whitewood boards. Pine boards are inexpensive, readily available, and forgiving to work with. As a softwood, pine is easier to cut and drill into. Any mistakes or misdrilled holes can easily be patched with wood filler, sanded, and painted over.

Ask at your local home improvement store for the pine or whitewood board sections. Look through the boards, selecting straight boards and avoiding knots, cracks, or twists. Since you will not have a scrap pile to pull from yet, buy an extra board to test cuts and joints on—or just in case you make a mistake.

Plan to paint your first project. Paint can hide just about anything!

plywood best—for example, you can get exactly four 1x12s or three 1x16s or two 1x24s from a full sheet of plywood.

If a project plan calls for a nonstandard-width board, I will provide details on how to cut these boards from sheet goods within each plan.

working with sheet goods

There are three main types of sheet goods traditionally used for in-home furnishings: hardwood plywood, medium density fiberboard (MDF), and particleboard.

HARDWOOD PLYWOOD Hardwood plywood is made up of several layers of wood, with the outer veneer a hardwood species. These species could be any wood species, from knotty alder to exotics including walnut and even bamboo; but birch, maple, and oak are most readily available. Hardwood plywood also can be purchased formaldehyde free, to avoid carcinogens being emitted in your home.

Hardwood plywood can be painted just like any other wood product, but you may find yourself reluctant to paint over the beautiful veneers. Staining hardwood plywood is a popular choice, but make sure you match other wood species to the veneer—for example, a maple veneer hardwood plywood would require maple trim boards for an even stain. You do have some flexibility, as some wood grains appear very similar, depending on the stain you choose. Clear grains like poplar work well with birch and maple plywood, but bamboo probably should not be paired with walnut. Use your best judgment, and always test finishes on scrap pieces to ensure an even and consistent finish.

The greatest challenge of hardwood plywood is the edges. When cut, the edges are exposed, and you will need to apply edge banding strips over raw edges for a stained finish. Edge banding is simply rolls of thin plywood veneer sized to cover exposed plywood edges. Applying edge banding is easy to do with a simple iron and a utility knife. But edge banding will add a slight amount of extra material to your project, altering dimensions, which could create problems later on, most notoriously on inset doors and drawer faces. Be aware of this if you are using edge banding.

An alternative to edge banding for painted projects is to fill exposed plywood edges with wood filler and sand them smooth. Do not leave exposed plywood edges unfinished. Paint alone will not cover the texture of unfinished edges.

MEDIUM DENSITY FIBERBOARD (MDF) MDF has become a retail standard for furniture because it is inexpensive, creates smooth finishes, and holds up well to moisture. MDF is a great choice for furniture you plan to paint.

However, MDF does have drawbacks. Most notably, MDF today is made with formaldehyde and can be harmful both to breathe while building and to the air quality of your home.

· MY BEST DIY TIPS & TRICKS ·

- Be superpicky about picking out straight boards.

- Boards are like cheese with a little mold at the corners: You can cut the imperfections off and the rest is still good.

- Make the longest cuts first. You'll get more out of your boards.

- Cut trim and face frames as you build, for the tightest fit.

- Save your scraps for future projects.

- Glue is cheap insurance.

- Sand and paint in the direction of the wood grain.

- Clamp everything.

- Take a break when you start making mistakes.

- Promise yourself that you will finish your current project before starting a new one.

- Wood filler and paint can hide just about anything.

- Enjoy the process.

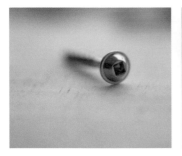

SCREWS

NAILS FOR FINISH NAILER

I find MDF also tends to split easily when you attach it at the edges. MDF works best with a pocket hole system and glue. But if you are attaching to the end grain, nails cause less splitting than screws. If you are using countersunk screws, never use wood screws with MDF because wood screw shafts taper, and this will cause your MDF to split or crack. Instead, opt for drywall screws, and carefully predrill holes with a pilot hole bit.

MDF edges should also be sanded smooth, and MDF must be primed before painting.

PARTICLEBOARD A big reason why I began building furniture so many years ago was that the only furniture I could afford to buy was made of particleboard. Particleboard does not hold up well, and it's difficult to build with, often splitting out. Particleboard acts like a sponge under moisture, absorbing and swelling, then falling apart. Most particleboard is made with adhesives containing formaldehyde.

But particleboard is inexpensive, roughly half the cost of MDF and one-third the cost of hardwood plywood. Though I do not recommend particleboard, many people choose to use it for the value.

FASTENERS

We have our boards; now we need a means to fasten them together to start assembling our furniture! There are two main types of fasteners used in this book: nails and screws. Each has a use in my shop, depending on the project and its intended use.

There are other means to join furniture, including mortise and tenons, biscuits, dowels, and complicated woodworking joints. For those readers with the advanced skill set and specialty tools for these types

of joints, all projects in this book can be easily modified for your preferred joinery method.

nails

I love nails. They are instant gratification for a builder. When a project is nailed with a finish nailer, all that's left to hide is a tiny nail hole.

But like anything quick and easy, nails have their drawbacks. The biggest drawback is the joint itself. Though strong enough for many applications, a nailed joint will not hold up under movement over time. Items such as chairs, benches and tables, projects that will be used for more than storage, should not be nailed.

But for projects that will not be subjected to constant movement and use—and in my home, abuse—nails are a great choice. Coupled with wood glue, a nailed joint will last. Once I made a mistake on a project and had to remove a board with a glued and nailed joint. I had to destroy the entire project because the glue held so tight that the actual board split before the joint gave.

Keep these common nail sizes on hand:
1¼" (3cm) nails • 2" (5cm) nails
I find myself using these nail sizes often when working with ¼" (6mm) plywood:
⅝" (16mm) nails • 1" (2.5cm) nails

wood glue

Wood glue is essential for creating a lasting joint. Glues today are so strong that projects often are made only with glue—without nails or screws! Choose a wood glue designed for working with unfinished wood, and use the wood glue to bond unfinished wood to unfinished wood. If you are working with painted projects, choose a wood glue designed to bond over finishes and carefully follow the directions.

Apply enough glue to form a thin layer on the joint, but avoid too much excess. Too much glue will seep out the sides of the joint and create ugly marks that are difficult to finish and won't take stain. Wipe excess glue off immediately with a damp cloth.

screws

I find myself using screws for most projects, especially screws made with a pocket hole joint. It is like having added insurance—not only is your joint secure and tight, but it is screwed together with threads, locking the joint indefinitely.

A screw also has the added ability to pull a joint tight as you fasten it, creating a better joint—something a nail cannot do.

Keep the following screw sizes on hand:

1¼" (3cm) pocket hole screws • 2½" (6.5cm) pocket hole screws • 1¼" (3cm) wood screws • 2" (5cm) wood screws • 2½" (6.5cm) wood screws • 3" (7.5cm) wood screws

Screws do have a downside: They are more difficult to hide, can split boards, and require the extra step of predrilling either a pocket hole or pilot hole. But for high-use projects, it's worth the extra work to assemble them with screws.

FINISHING SUPPLIES

A nice finish can make a good project great or ruin it. Having the right materials to finish your project is a small investment that makes a big difference.

After you finish building your project, you may look at it in dismay, thinking that it looks nothing like the photo in the book! But have faith; all of those holes will disappear, and with a little more work, the wood will look so smooth that you will wonder whether you even want to paint it!

wood filler

Think of wood filler as the concealer or cover-up you add before you put foundation on. When applied to

imperfections in the wood, wood filler hides holes and blends well, becoming invisible under paint or stain.

For painted projects, you can use any type of wood filler. I prefer tubs of wood filler rather than tubes of wood filler, so I can dip my putty knife into it. Others prefer using tubes because wood filler dries out fast, and tubes tend to keep longer.

For stained projects, I've had success with stainable wood filler, but be sure to test the stain with the filler on a piece of scrap wood—the stainable wood filler may work with some stains and not so great with others.

Often wood stains are paired with prestained wood fillers in coordinating colors. This is an easy way to know you are getting a perfect match, so these wood fillers can be worth buying, especially for darker stains.

PAINTED FINISH

Painted furniture is by far my most favorite. I find that one bright red armoire or a daring turquoise farmhouse table can make a room. It can offer the same punch as bold shoes or a vibrant handbag.

Painting a piece of furniture is also easier than painting an entire room—and much less risky to redo if you are not satisfied.

Knowing a little about paints now will save you hours in the paint aisle later.

primer

Priming a project is important because it bonds the paint with the wood. It also seals the wood, so tannins in the wood do not later come out and discolor your finish.

Primer also acts as that first coat of paint, and with primer being less expensive than paint, it will ultimately save you money. I find taking the extra step to prime projects results in a more even finish and fewer coats of paint.

Purchase primer in gallons, as you will use primer for a variety of projects. Choose a primer designed for the application.

paint

What true do-it-yourselfer does not love the paint aisle? It is so full of possibilities!

But with all those possibilities come choices. Paint comes in different sheens—flat, eggshell, satin, semigloss, and high gloss. All sheens, except for flat, typically have enamel, so if you use a flat paint remember to protect it with a top coat.

I love working with flat paint. It goes on furniture smoothly and you can layer coat after coat without creating a gooey mess. As you move upward in sheen, the paint gets thicker and takes longer to dry. I prefer using a thinner paint and adding more coats for a deeper finish, and I've also found multiple layers of paint will hide scratches better than one thick coat.

But that said, I have had great success with most all types of paints, and the desired finished project should dictate the type of paint you purchase. The higher the sheen, the fewer coats needed, which can result in a less time-consuming finishing process.

For exterior applications, always choose exterior grade paints. These paints have UV filters and will not fade as fast as interior paint.

top coat

Top coats are usually clear and are meant to protect your finish. They will make your furniture wipe clean and give it a smooth sheen. For paints with enamels, you may not need it.

There are many different types of top coat, ranging from oil-based to latex and even shellac (made from insect shells). There are spray-on, brush-on, and even rub-on wax coatings.

The most important decision in choosing a top coat is finding one that works with your paint and for your applications. Some top coats are so strong that they can take the finish right off of your project! Others might not bond, making a splotchy mess of your finish. It is important to read the can; make sure that your top coat works well with your paint.

TIP Most paint counters are staffed with very knowledgeable and helpful people. Do not be shy about asking questions; they will certainly be happier to hear your questions now than your complaints later!

STAINED FINISH

In a home where everything is painted, sometimes a little wood grain can give a nice touch of warmth. Stained wood has such character and depth, many people prefer it to paint. Also, stain tends to hold up better to use, hiding scratches better than paint.

But it is often more difficult to achieve a rich, even stain. And unlike paint, mistakes are not as easy as just adding an extra coat. It is often very difficult if not impossible to remove wood stain once applied, so it is important to choose the right staining materials for your project.

wood conditioner

Wood conditioner is applied prior to wood stain to assist in a more even application. Depending on the type of wood you are staining, with softwoods being more susceptible to blotchiness, you may wish to use a wood conditioner.

I always test first. Wood and how it accepts stain can vary from species to species, even from board to board. To test, stain a piece of scrap wood from the project. If the stain applies evenly, wood conditioner is not necessary. If the stain appears blotchy and uneven, invest in wood conditioner.

stain

Like paint, stain comes in many different colors and types. Wood stain also comes in gels, creams, and traditional liquid forms.

Gel and cream stains tend to provide a richer, more even coverage but are more expensive. Traditional stains are easier to apply and less expensive, but I find it more difficult to achieve professional-looking results with them.

Cream stains can be used as glazes for adding depth to distressed finishes.

If you are unsure of the type of stain to use, ask for a sample or purchase a small container and test out the stains for the result you want prior to using. Most stains will require a top coat to protect the finish. Ensure your top coat is suitable for your stain type

staining rags or brush

Often you will need rags or a brush to apply stain. Read the instructions on your stain, if your stain is oil based, you may not be able to clean the brush after using it for staining.

HARDWARE AND ACCESSORIES

Hardware adds more than functionality to a project. Hardware is also the jewelry on your project, and it can upgrade a simple cabinet to contemporary sophistication or turn it into a warm country find.

knobs and handles

There are thousands and thousands of options for knobs and handles out there for your project. Take time

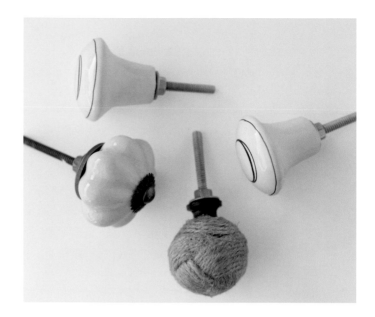

to pick out handles or knobs that you love; they will enhance your project. Some of my favorite projects are the most basic with simple white finishes and beautiful hardware.

hinges

While having a good selection of knobs and handles literally opens up a world of possibilities, it can also be slightly overwhelming. My favorite hinges are the non-mortise Euro-style hinges, because they install invisibly for inset and full-overlay doors with just a drill! In this book, recommendations on the exact types of hinges are given for all plans requiring them.

drawer slides

Drawer slides, when used properly, are your friend. They not only take the complexity out of installing drawers but ensure they will slide smoothly and evenly.

My favorite type is an inexpensive, white Euro-style drawer slide. These drawer slides go on the bottom corners of your drawers, holding the bottom in place while creating the sliding mechanics for your drawers.

Standard off-the-shelf drawer slides come in widths of 14" (35.5cm) and greater. Smaller 12" (30.5cm) drawer slides are available by special order, but at that short length, a drawer slide fashioned of wood and coated with wax usually will suffice. For projects requiring drawer slides, I provide additional details and recommendations.

caster wheels

These are simply wheels attached to a base that can be easily screwed to the bottom of your project. Caster wheels come in many different sizes and styles. Most have a base plate for easy installation, but some are designed to fit in a drilled hole. Check to make sure the caster wheels you purchase include screws, or you will need to purchase screws.

catches and clasps

Sometimes your doors need a little something extra to stay closed. Catches or clasps are inexpensive and easy to install. Magnetic clasps work well for most cabinet doors, but catches can provide a more secure hold.

Check out this coat storage shelf with hooks, on page 32. I love adding hooks to projects to create instant easy storage. Another trick? House numbers can add charm and character to a piece.

This bench is also handbuilt. Visit ana-white.com for the plans.

·2·
BASIC TECHNIQUES

To me, building is much like cooking or sewing or any other craft.

You don't have to be a master chef to make a wonderful dinner any more than you need to be a professional woodworker in a top-notch workshop to make beautiful furniture. There are just a few simple steps that make up most of the work. And if you can master these steps, you will consistently produce good results.

preparation

UNDERSTANDING PLANS

In this book, plans follow the same format. Each plan includes a Shopping List to help you determine the materials you will need for each project. It's always a good idea to keep a scrap pile and pull from there before investing in new materials in order to keep projects as inexpensive as possible.

The plans also include a Cutting List, giving you full instruction on the length each board needs to be cut.

For most projects, you will need to have the basic hand tools, including a tape measure, a square, a level, drill bits, screwdrivers, a carpenter's pencil, safety equipment, clamps, and a pocket hole jig. Each project then lists the specific power tools that you will need to complete the project.

In addition to having basic tools on hand, you

will also need basic materials called for in most every project. These materials include glue, sandpaper, paint, primer or finishing supplies, and wood filler. It's a good idea to have a paint drop cloth, blue painter's tape, and scrap wood in varying sizes available to assist you when building or to elevate a project when painting.

Projects are then listed as either Starter, Beginner, Intermediate, or Advanced. Each project has a detailed dimensions diagram. Use this diagram to understand the size of the project.

The project plans themselves are formatted in a step-by-step manner, with diagrams depicting each step. You do not necessarily have to follow the steps exactly, especially as your skill level increases—for example, you may decide to build a face frame first and then nail it on instead of nailing the face frame on board by board—but it is recommended that you read through the project and understand fully how the project is put together before you begin.

Once you have familiarized yourself with the plan and acquired the necessary tools, it's time to prepare for building. As mentioned earlier (page 15), creating dedicated stations for each task will save you time and frustration. Gather your tools and keep them within easy reach. Make sure your space is clean and level. Put on your safety equipment, and let us begin!

cutting

The first step in building the actual project is cutting. First look over the project's Cutting List in detail. Read through the plan and note any angled or curved cuts, taking into account long-point or short-point measurements. Plan your cuts to minimize waste of boards. A good practice is to draw out your boards on graph paper and mark cuts on paper before cutting. You can choose to cut all your boards at once or cut as you go, depending on your workspace. I personally like to cut all of the main box boards first and then cut the trim and face frame boards for the most precise fit. This book does not provide cutting layouts on most projects, because you will most likely be pulling from your scrap pile with nonstandard-length boards after your first project.

TIP It is always a good rule to make your longest cuts first, working your way down to the smallest.

· WHAT IS A CUTTING LIST? ·

Think of a cutting list as the ingredients list in a recipe. It is organized as boards appear in the plan, first giving the quantity needed, followed by the length to cut to, the type of board, and a description of the board. For metric conversions of standard measurements used in this book, refer to the chart at the back.

CUTTING LIST

2 16"-long **1x10s** (sides)

1 48"-long **1x10** (top)

1 46½"-long **1x10** (bottom shelf)

RIPPING

If you are working on a project that uses nonstandard-width boards, or you choose to use sheet goods for boards, you will need to rip the board to size. Ripping, or cutting a board down to size in the direction of the grain, should be the first cuts made, as you want the width cut to be consistent from board to board. Most home improvement stores will make complimentary cuts for you. Ask to have your plywood cut into strips as directed in the plan. This will make hauling plywood much easier, too.

If you are ripping your own plywood, you will need to use either a table saw or a circular saw. For ripping with a table saw, carefully set your table saw fence to the desired width using your tape measure. Have someone help you run the wood through the table saw. This is a two-person task, as one person will feed the plywood through and the other person will catch the plywood as it is passed through the table saw.

TIP Before ripping your wood, run a scrap piece of plywood through the table saw, and check the cut width for accuracy.

For ripping with a circular saw, mark the cut with a chalk line. Adjust your circular saw blade for the thickness of the wood. Support all parts of the wood so that your saw blade does not get pinched as you cut. And remember: You need to measure each cut as you go, because as you cut, sawdust is created, resulting in loss material, altering measurements.

CROSSCUTS OR SQUARE CUTS

Crosscuts or square cuts are used to cut a board to the size needed. A crosscut is perpendicular to the length of the board at a straight 90-degree angle, usually across the grain. It is always good practice to first square up the end of your boards by making a quick crosscut at the very end, since you cannot assume they are already square. At the very least, check factory ends for square using your carpentry square.

TIP Never trust a factory-cut end of a board, but always trust a factory edge of sheet goods.

❏ Review cut list and understand each board's use and placement.

❏ Create a cutting layout on graph paper.

❏ Rip any sheet goods to consistent widths.

❏ Note any angled or curved cuts.

❏ Begin cutting longest boards first.

❏ Check cuts for accurate lengths.

❏ Cut angled cuts, testing to make sure angles are accurate.

❏ For curved cuts, create a pattern and make curved cuts from the pattern.

❏ Reserve molding cuts to fit project.

If you are cutting with a handheld saw (circular saw or jigsaw), measure the cut from the squared-up end and mark. Use your speed square to draw a line at the mark perpendicular to the board length. Considering the width of your saw blade, cut the board along the outside edge of the marked line. Measure your cut to make sure it is accurate to the cut list.

If you are using a miter saw, chop saw, or other fixed saw, measure the length of the cut, hold the board flush to fence on the saw, and make your cut. On your first cuts, take a second to measure and confirm that your cuts are accurate in length.

TIP When measuring cuts, keep your tape measure parallel to the edge of the board. Measurements taken at an angle will not be accurate.

ANGLED CUTS

Making an angled cut is not too different from making a square cut. You are still cutting a straight line across the grain. It is the marking of angle cuts that will take a little extra effort. If you have a miter saw or compound miter saw or other fixed saw that cuts angles, simply set your saw at the correct angle as directed in the project plan and cut.

Angles in project plans are given as an "off-square" angle. A crosscut or square cut always measures 90 degrees, or perpendicular to the board edge. Off square is measured as degrees from the square cut. For example, if the plan calls for a 10-degree off-square cut, the angle itself to the board edge would be 80 degrees or 100 degrees, figured by adding or subtracting 10 degrees off of square, which is 90 degrees.

So first measure the board and mark the cut to the measurement given as you would a square cut. Use a compass to measure and mark degrees off square. and then draw a line between the measurement and the angle mark.

All angled cuts in this book are noted as long-point or short-point measurements. When you make an angled cut, one end will be the longer end—meaning it will measure longer—and the other will be the shorter end. Pay attention to long-point and short-point measurements as you cut; it will determine what direction the cut is made off of square.

TIP It is very important to make accurate angled cuts. A project can become greatly out of square even if you are just a few degrees off.

CURVED CUTS

In this book, curved cuts are mostly used for decorative purposes—to soften the lines of a project or to create interest. For the best success with curved cuts, carefully mark out the cut on scrap board. Secure a scrap to your workbench and carefully cut the curve with your saw, considering the width of the saw blade as you cut, cutting to either the inside or the outside of the line.

When you have made a curved cut you are happy with, use it as a pattern to make cuts on your project. Always use the same pattern for all cuts, and consider saw-blade placement as you cut. For example, always cut to the inside of your pattern marks, or always cut to the outside of your pattern mark, for the most consistent cuts from board to board.

In most cases, curved cuts will require sanding. Sand with coarse sandpaper followed by medium grit until the cuts are smooth and, if you made multiple cuts from the same pattern, identical. For multiple cuts from the same pattern, consider clamping all cut edges together and sanding them as a stack to create the most consistent edges.

building

This is my favorite part! We've prepared, prepped, and cut, and now it's time to actually build your project! If you follow these steps, you will be confident and cruise right through the building process.

❶ MARKING JOINTS

Taking a few minutes to mark your joints prior to actually building will help you put your project together more accurately. Make a dry run of the plans, marking all joints with a square, as outlined in the plans. This dry run will also give you a good understanding of how the project is assembled.

❷ MARKING SCREW HOLES

If you are screwing your project together, you will want to predrill all holes. As you go through your dry run and mark joints, take a second to also mark the location of all screws. If you are using pocket holes, this is especially important, as drilling a pocket hole can be very difficult once you have started assembly. Predrill all of your screws prior to building, with screws placed every 6" (15cm) to 8" (20.5cm) and screws on each end of the joint.

❸ ASSEMBLING

nailing

Once your joints are marked, apply glue to the joint, and line up the two boards as directed in the project plan. A good rule is to use the longest nail possible without going through the second board. Clamp boards when possible. Keep your fingers away from the joint so you don't accidentally injure them with a stray nail.

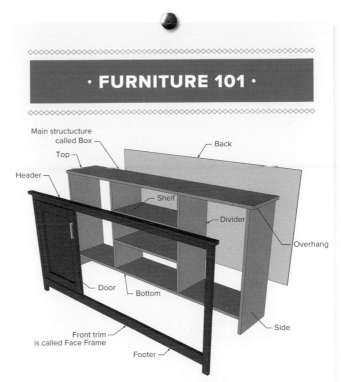

• FURNITURE 101 •

For me, understanding how simple a piece of furniture actually is was instrumental in building my confidence to tackle projects. Most furniture is constructed in the following manner: You start by building a box that makes up the basic shape of your project. Then you add a back. This is followed by a face frame comprised of trim boards. From here, you can add doors or drawers to further enhance the form and function of your project.

BOX Also called the carcass, the box is the basic shape of your project, usually constructed from wider-width boards or plywood.

BACK Most commonly ¼" (6mm) plywood cut to shape and then glued and nailed to the back of the box. The back adds considerable strength and stability to projects.

FACE FRAME A face frame is a group of boards added to the front of the box to create a finished front to projects. The face frame also adds considerable strength, conceals plywood edges, and often supports hardware for doors and drawers. Face frames are not essential to a project.

· HOW TO PREDRILL A PILOT HOLE ·

Apply glue and clamp the two boards you will be joining together in place. Load the drill with a countersinking drill bit, making sure the drill bit is about the same length and thickness as your screw. The countersinking part of the drill bit needs to be sized larger than the screw head. Drill a pilot hole through both boards, keeping the drill straight and square as you predrill, until you have a large enough hole to hide the screw head below the surface of wood. Swap the countersink bit out for a driving bit to match your screw heads and drive screws into the wood, creating the joint. Remove the clamps, and wipe off any excess glue.

Apply firm, even pressure and nail your joint. Nails should be spaced every 6" (15cm) to 8" (20.5cm), and on the beginning and end of every joint.

countersinking

With your joints marked and your holes predrilled, countersinking should be as easy as applying glue and driving screws. It is still a good idea to clamp boards, and you also may need to predrill pilot holes in the second board to avoid splitting, especially near the ends. Carefully insert your screws. If the board begins to split, remove the screw, and predrill a pilot hole. Self-tapping screws, screws with a tiny sharp edge at the tip that predrill a pilot hole as they are driven, though more expensive, can reduce board splitting and save you time.

POCKET HOLES Using a countersink drill bit creates the challenge of exposed screw holes and also requires additional steps. Often, you will need to attach through the end grain with a countersink bit, not always the strongest method of joinery.

A pocket hole attaches at an angle from the underside, hiding the screw holes. The pocket hole jig simplifies the steps necessary and creates a stronger joint, because you are hooking into the grain of the wood.

When you are building with pocket holes, it is very important that you drill all pocket holes prior to assembly. Go through the project after cutting, and mark each and every pocket hole. One of my tricks with pocket holes is to put them either where they are completely hidden or where they are easy to finish.

When assembling furniture with pocket holes, glue and clamp the joint. Then slowly insert the screw and begin to drive the screw. If you notice the second board splitting, back the screw out, and drive again, just slightly deeper. Do this until the screw is fully inserted.

Sometimes angling your pocket holes in a different direction to further grab into the second board can reduce splitting and increase the strength of your joint.

Refer to the instructions that accompany your pocket hole jig for further information that may be more specific to your type of pocket hole jig.

4 CHECKING FOR SQUARE

As you assemble your project, take a second after each step to ensure your project is square. If a project is square, the diagonal measurements from opposite corners will match up. If the opposing diagonals do not match, push the two corners with the longer measurement together until square.

finishing

Once the project is completely assembled, it's time to finish it. Finishing is always a little scary; you have put so much time and effort into your project, you do not want to mess it up now! Follow these simple instructions to achieve a finish worthy of your beautiful project.

FILLING HOLES

No doubt, building your project has left a screw hole or two showing, and maybe an imperfection that you could live without. Use your putty knife to fill all holes with wood filler, overfilling the holes. Note that wood filler can shrink as it dries, so for larger holes you will need to apply a second or possibly more coats of wood filler.

Let the wood filler dry completely between coats. If not completely dried, the wood filler will come off in chunks as you sand.

SANDING

Once the wood filler has dried completely, begin sanding with coarse-grit sandpaper. Sand your project in the direction of the wood grain, evening out joints and removing excess wood filler. Follow the initial coarse-grit sanding with medium-grit sandpaper, sanding the entire project in the direction of the wood grain. Finish with fine-grit sandpaper if necessary for your type of finish.

If you notice any imperfections or holes, apply another round of wood filler. It's easier to get it right now than later. Repeat the sanding process.

PREPARING FOR PAINT OR STAIN

After you finish sanding, your project is now covered with sawdust. Vacuum the entire project with a soft bristled brush, removing all sawdust and debris from the project. Do the same for your work surface to avoid sawdust in your paint.

With a slightly damp rag, wipe the project clean, removing any remaining sawdust particles from the project. Remember, you are only removing sawdust, and don't want to soak your wood, as that will affect your finish. Let your project dry completely.

PAINTING OR STAINING

If it looks good au naturel, it's going to look great finished!

Before you paint or stain, take a second to test out the finish on a scrap piece of wood. The time to make adjustments is before, not after, you paint. If you are happy with the results, it's go time.

With the project elevated to your height, preferably on a workbench, turn the project upside down and paint from the center outward. This way you can avoid covering your sleeves in paint or, at the very least, creating difficulties with painting tight spots. A good rule is to paint the hardest-to-reach places first. Let dry.

· YOUR FIRST PROJECT ·

Starting anything new can be challenging and overwhelming—building furniture especially so, because likely everything is new. I promise you, you will make mistakes. You will get discouraged. And in the end, you might describe your first project as far from perfect.

But after all of these years, it is the first imperfect projects that I cherish the most. I do not obsess over the drawers not lining up or sliding correctly, or nitpick the gaps between joints. Instead, I look at the project as a whole and think with pride: I made that.

On your first project, begin with an open mind. Be open to making mistakes and learning how to fix them. Often, my happiest moments in the garage are when I finally figure out how to overcome a mistake. It is like reaching the top of a hill when you are running. You might doubt yourself when you are still battling to get uphill, but once there, you will thank yourself for sticking it out.

But there are things you can do to set yourself up for success. Choose an easy project. Educate yourself by reading through the plans several times and reviewing each step, gaining confidence and understanding. Do not be shy about asking for help, whether that means reaching out to other builders or asking a friend to hold a few boards. Remember, you are learning something new, so keep an open mind and an optimistic spirit, and you will surprise yourself with success.

Once dry, flip your project over and repeat the painting process, starting with the most difficult-to-reach places first, working your way outward. Apply as many coats as necessary to achieve your desired finish, as directed on your paint or stain cans.

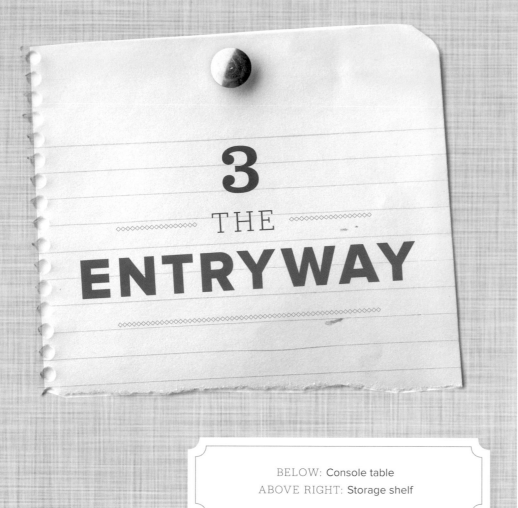

3
THE
ENTRYWAY

BELOW: Console table
ABOVE RIGHT: Storage shelf

A tidy and organized entryway has two very important tasks:

It is a transition point for the family, storing everything from umbrellas to coats to mail. And it is the first impression of a home, giving guests and family alike a snapshot of your entire house.

I've included in this chapter plans that will help you create an entryway that will both work hard and wow guests. While these projects pack tons of functionality perfect for a tiny entryway, all of these pieces can be used in any room of your home.

STORAGE SHELF
with coat hooks

SHOPPING LIST

1	8'-long **1x10**
1	6'-long **1x10**
1	4'-long **1x8**
1	8'-long **1x2**
¼	sheet of ¼" plywood

Wood glue

1¼" finish nails

2" finish nails

3" screws (for hanging) or heavy-duty shelf-hanging kit

3 hooks

Finishing supplies

TOOLS

Basic hand tools

Circular saw

Jigsaw

Finish nailer

CUTTING LIST

2	16"-long **1x10s** (sides)
1	48"-long **1x10** (top)
1	46½"-long **1x10** (bottom shelf)
2	8"-long **1x10s** (dividers)
1	46½"-long **1x8** (hook back)
1	17½" x 48" piece of ¼" plywood (back)
1	49½"-long **1x2** (top front crown)
2	8¾"-long **1x2s** (top side crowns)

YOU WILL BE PLEASANTLY SURPRISED to discover how much organization this simple storage shelf can bring to your home. Featuring three large cubbies, three coat hooks, and storage on top, you can hang it low for children to put their own backpacks away. Or hang it higher for adults and set a bench under it to create a mudroom on a budget.

DIMENSIONS

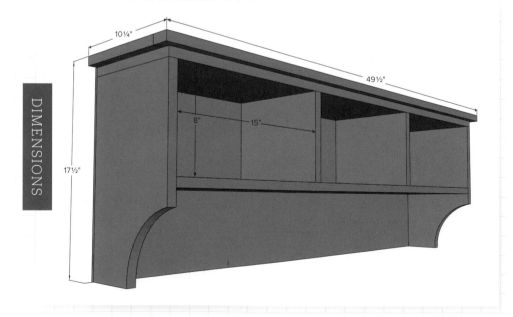

· FINISHING ·

I wanted a smooth, even finish for the storage shelf with hooks. To achieve this, I used medium-grit sandpaper on the project until very smooth. Primer was sprayed on and allowed to dry, and then two coats of semigloss black paint were sprayed on. The smooth finish has held up well to constant use in our entryway.

1 ENDS

On the two side pieces cut in the cutting list, trace an arch to the measurements shown in the diagram. Using the jigsaw, carefully cut out the arch in one continuous cut. Repeat on the other piece. Clamp both pieces together, with all four sides flush, and sand the arches until smooth and matching.

2 BOX

Attach the top piece to the sides with wood glue and 2" (5cm) finish nails or screws. Measure and mark the placement of the bottom shelf as shown in the diagram. Join the bottom shelf to the sides with glue and 2" (5cm) finish nails. Check for square and adjust if necessary.

3 DIVIDERS

Measure and mark the placement of dividers on both the top piece and shelf. Position dividers inside the shelf and attach with glue and 2" (5cm) finish nails.

4 HOOK BACK

Apply glue to top and side edges of the 1x8 hook back board. Fit it in the shelf box and nail with 2" (5cm) finish nails on top and sides.

5 BACK

Apply glue to the edges of the back, and place the ¼" (6mm) plywood piece on. Attach with 1¼" (3cm) finish nails.

6 FRONT CROWN

Apply glue to top edge of shelf. Place the top front crown on the shelf, overhanging the front and sides by ¾" (2cm). Join with 1¼" (3cm) finish nails.

7 SIDE CROWN

Apply glue to the back sides of the top side crown pieces. Place the top side crowns on the project, flush with outside corner of the top front crown. Join with 1¼" (3cm) finish nails.

8 HANGING

The storage shelf with coat hooks can be hung directly through the hook support into a stud in your wall, or you can use a purchased heavy-duty hanging system. Make sure your shelf is firmly hung and attached to at least two studs in the wall.

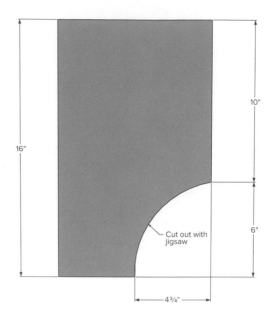

1

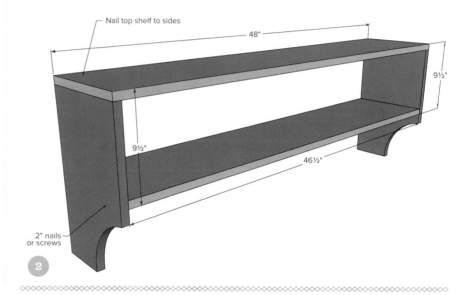

2

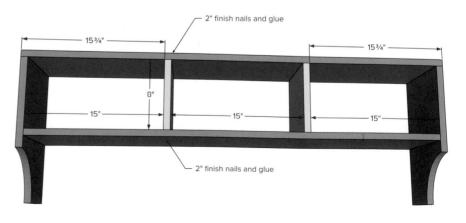

3

TIP Space coat hooks every $11^5/_8$" for 3 coat hooks, centered on your $1/_8$", $3^1/_8$" up from base of shelf. Predrill holes and attach with screws accompanying the coat hooks.

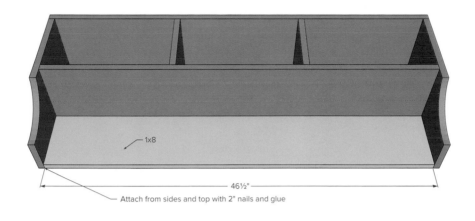

1x8

46½"

Attach from sides and top with 2" nails and glue

4

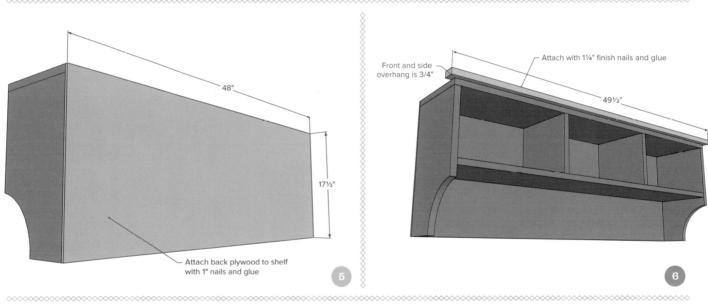

48"

17½"

Attach back plywood to shelf with 1" nails and glue

5

Front and side overhang is 3/4"

Attach with 1¼" finish nails and glue

49½"

6

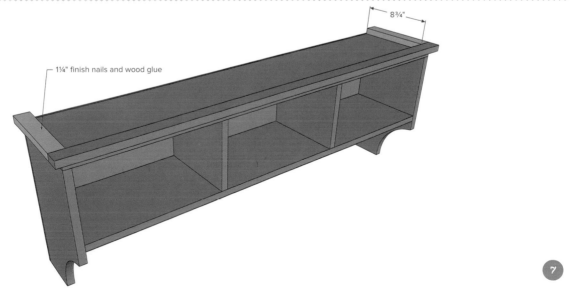

8¾"

1¼" finish nails and wood glue

7

PROJECT
Nº 2
MIRROR

A MIRROR CAN MAKE YOUR ENTRYWAY appear larger and give you one last chance to fix your hair before heading out the door. With three hooks and two shelves—one on top and one perfect for a decorative candle, your mail, or a photo of your loved ones— this mirror is also superfunctional.

SHOPPING LIST

- **1** 6'-long 1x6
- **1** 10'-long 1x4
- **8** 1¼" pocket hole screws
- 2" finish nails
- Wood glue
- **1** 24" x 30" mirror
- Clear epoxy glue or mirror clips
- Heavy-duty picture-frame hanging kit
- **3** coat hooks
- Finishing supplies

TOOLS

- Basic hand tools
- Pocket hole jig
- Jigsaw
- Sandpaper with sanding block or power sander
- Circular saw or miter saw (for making straight cuts)
- Finish nailer

CUTTING LIST

- **2** 29"-long **1x4s** (sides)
- **2** 28"-long **1x6s** (bottom and bottom shelf)
- **2** 28"-long **1x4s** (top and top shelf)
- **2** 2¾"-long **1x4s** (top-shelf supports)
- **2** 4¾"-long **1x6s** (bottom-shelf supports)

DIMENSIONS

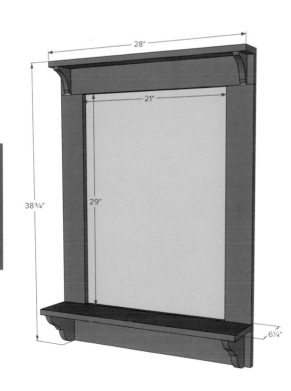

1 BASE FRAME

On each end of the 1x4 side pieces, drill two pocket holes with a pocket hole jig set for ¾" (2cm) thick boards (normally 1x boards). Then carefully attach a 1x6 board to the bottom with 1¼" (3cm) pocket hole screws, and one 1x4 board to the top with 1¼" (3cm) pocket hole screws.

2 TOP-SHELF SUPPORTS

On the 1x4 top-shelf support pieces, draw and cut out an arch shape with a jigsaw. Sand the cut until smooth and both supports match. Line the supports up with the top of the mirror, 1" (2.5cm) in from the sides of mirror frame, and join with wood glue and 2" (5cm) finish nails.

3 TOP SHELF

Attach the 1x4 top shelf to both shelf supports and the top of the mirror frame with wood glue and 2" (5cm) finish nails.

4 BOTTOM SUPPORTS

Using a jigsaw, cut bottom supports as shown in the diagram, and sand the cut edges until smooth and both supports match. From the back, fasten the bottom supports 1" (2.5cm) in from the side edges of mirror frame, flush with the bottom, using wood glue and 2" (5cm) finish nails.

5 BOTTOM SHELF

Attach the bottom shelf to the bottom supports with wood glue and 2" (5cm) finish nails. Nail through the back as well.

6 MIRROR AND HARDWARE

It's best at this stage to dry-fit the mirror, testing to make sure the mirror fits well in the frame. Once satisfied that your mirror fits, set the mirror aside. Sand and paint the frame in the desired color. Then clean the mirror and the back of the frame. Using clear epoxy glue, adhere the mirror to the frame. Attach mounting hardware and hooks to the back. (The mirror can also be held in place with mirror clips, readily available and inexpensive hardware used to secure mirrors to walls or frames.)

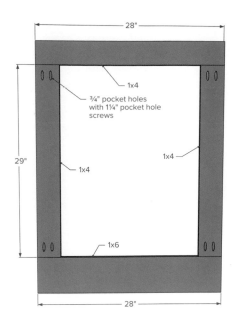

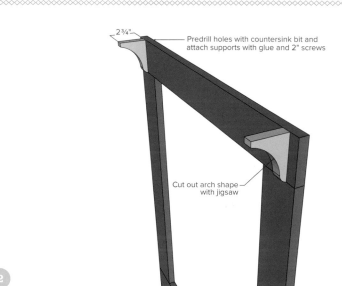

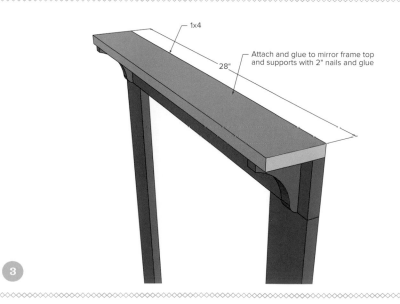

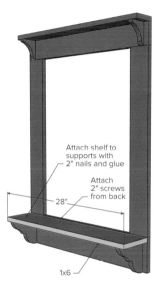

5½"

2½"

2½"

3"

Cut out decorative scallop shape
from 1x6 support pieces

Attach with
2" screws
and glue
from back

4

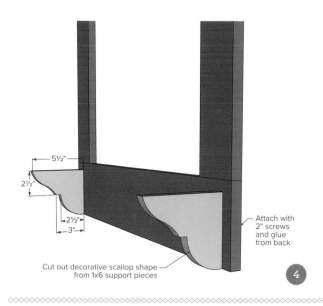

Attach shelf to
supports with
2" nails and glue

Attach
2" screws
from back

28"

1x6

5

Attach mounting hardware

24"

30"

Glue mirror on frame or use mirror clips

6

· FINISHING ·

I lightly sanded any rough edges, joints, and the cuts made with the jigsaw but left the wood imperfect and rustic. The frame was primed with white primer, followed by one coat of French blue semigloss paint. I let the paint dry for a full day. Then where the wood was imperfect, paint was scraped off with a wood chisel, giving the project a distressed look. I also did some extra sanding on high-wear areas to give the distressing a more authentic appearance. Finally, a clear top coat was applied to protect the finish. I used a picture-hanging kit to hang the mirror on the wall.

PROJECT
Nº 3

CONSOLE TABLE

I REMEMBER MAKING THIS CONSOLE table for the first time and just loving how it turned out. Sturdy, full of character, yet inexpensive to make, this console can be used to stylishly keep small items such as keys or sunglasses within easy reach. The shelf is the perfect place to add baskets to help organize anything from recycling to shoes, or just use it to show off your favorite books. We will see how versatile this piece is later when we add a hutch (page 81).

SHOPPING LIST

1	8'-long 1x2
1	8'-long 1x3
2	8'-long 1x4s
1	4'-long 1x6
1	10'-long 1x12
5	8'-long 2x2s
¼	sheet of ¼" plywood

Wood glue
1¼" finish nails
2" finish nails
1¼" pocket hole screws
2½" pocket hole screws or 2" countersink screws
2" screws

2	sets of 12" Euro-style drawer slides (inexpensive white ones)
2	knobs or handles

Finishing supplies

TOOLS

Basic hand tools

Pocket hole jig or drill with countersink drill bits

Circular saw or other saw for making crosscuts

Finish nailer

CUTTING LIST

4	11¼"-long **1x2s** (side trim)
2	8¾"-long **1x12s** (side aprons)
4	29¼"-long **2x2s** (legs)
6	39"-long **2x2s** (front/back trim)
2	5¾"-long **2x2s** (drawer dividers)
1	42" x 8¾" piece of ¼" plywood (back)
4	11¼"-long **2x2s** (supports)
1	46"-long **1x12** (top)
1	42"-long **1x12** (bottom shelf)
1	46"-long **1x2** (trim, back)
1	46"-long **1x3** (trim, front)

DRAWERS

4	16¼"-long **1x4s** (drawer fronts/backs)
4	13"-long **1x4s** (drawer sides)
2	17¾" x 13" pieces of ¼" plywood (drawer bottoms)
2	18½"-long **1x6s** (drawer faces)

DIMENSIONS

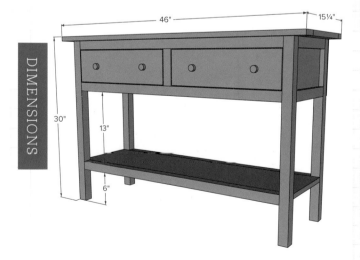

46"
15¼"
30"
13"
6"

NOTE

It is very important to drill all pocket holes before beginning, so go through the plan, mark each board for pocket hole locations, drill the holes, and only then begin assembly.

Make a matching hutch!
See plans on page 80.

· BUILT BY ·
ASHLEY MILLS

http://www.thehandmadehome.net/

" My husband and I knocked this project out in a weekend. Quite the versatile piece, this great console table, with the matching hutch, really is a simple project, even for the beginner. Every piece of wood can be cut by the lumberyard, and the only tools you need, at a minimum: a hammer, screw gun, and pocket hole jig. The trickiest part of the whole project was making sure we kept everything level and square. This is where that second pair of hands made it much easier. "

1 SIDE TRIM

Attach the side-trim boards to the side piece with wood glue and 1¼" (3cm) nails, keeping outside edges flush. Note that if your 1x12 is not 11¼" (28.5cm) wide, you will need to adjust the length of your trim board to the width of your 1x12 board.

2 LEGS

Drill ¾" (2cm) pocket holes. Using 1¼" (3cm) pocket hole screws, attach the legs to the side aprons of the project. Keep the top and sides flush. You can also join with glue and 2½" (6.5cm) countersunk screws. You will need to build two.

3 FRONT/BACK TRIM

Drill 1½" (3.8cm) pocket holes on each end of the front/back trim boards and attach to the legs as shown in the diagram. Use glue on all joints. Start at the top and work your way down, with the project turned upside down for best results and easiest access to pocket holes. You can also join with glue and 2½" (6.5cm) countersunk screws.

4 DRAWER DIVIDERS

Mark the placement of the drawer divider, centered on the table as shown in the diagram. Fasten in place with either 2½" (6.5cm) pocket hole screws from the inside or 2½" (6.5cm) countersunk screws from the top and bottom.

5 BACK

Attach the back to the console table with wood glue and 1¼" (3cm) finish nails.

6 SUPPORTS

Supports can be attached either with 2½" (6.5cm) pocket hole screws or 2½" (6.5cm) countersunk screws. Mark the placement and fasten with glue and screws. Note that the bottom support must be flush to bottom of drawer divider; we will fasten the drawer slides to this board.

7 TOP

Using glue and 2" (5cm) screws, attach the top to the supports, leaving 1¾" (4.5cm) overhangs on both ends. Note the 1x12 top fits even with the side trim.

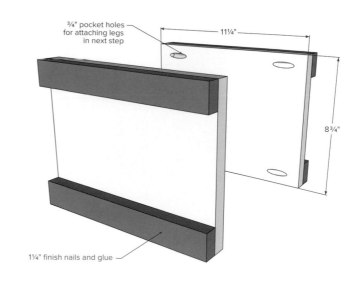

¾" pocket holes for attaching legs in next step

11¼"

8¾"

1¼" finish nails and glue

1

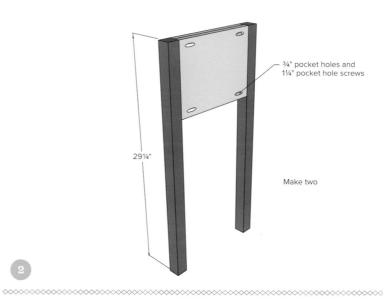

¾" pocket holes and 1¼" pocket hole screws

29¼"

Make two

2

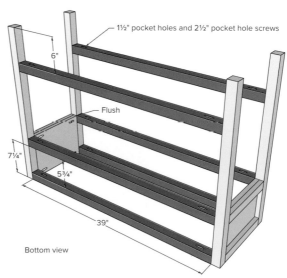

1½" pocket holes and 2½" pocket hole screws

6"

Flush

7¼"

5¾"

39"

Bottom view

3

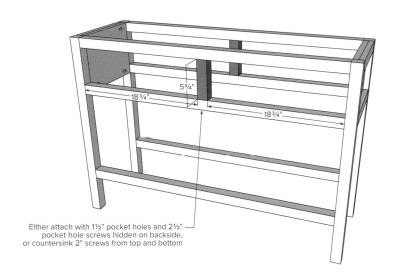

5¾"

18¾"

18¾"

Either attach with 1½" pocket holes and 2½"
pocket hole screws hidden on backside,
or countersink 2" screws from top and bottom

4

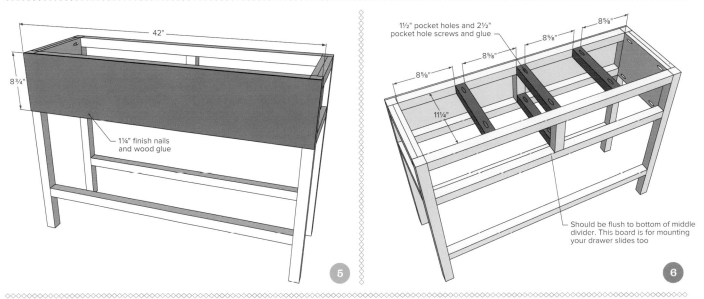

42"

8¾"

1¼" finish nails
and wood glue

5

1½" pocket holes and 2½"
pocket hole screws and glue

8⅝"

8⅝"

8⅝"

8⅝"

11¼"

Should be flush to bottom of middle
divider. This board is for mounting
your drawer slides too

6

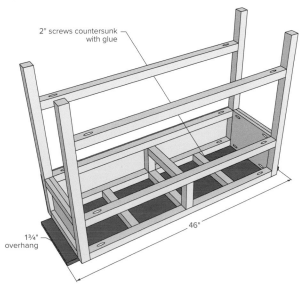

2" screws countersunk
with glue

1¾"
overhang

46"

7

8 BOTTOM SHELF

Clamp bottom shelf, if necessary. Either drill ¾" pocket holes along both edges of the bottom shelf and screw it to the bottom shelf trim with 1¼" pocket hole screws, or attach with glue and 2½" (6.5cm) countersunk screws. Ends should be flush to the outsides of the legs.

9 TOP TRIM

Attach the 1x3 and 1x2 trim boards with glue, and nail it down with 2" (5cm) nails. Note the 1x2 is on the back and the 1x3 is on the front. Keep the outsides flush.

10 DRAWERS

Build drawer boxes and attach the bottoms with glue and 1¼" (3cm) finish nails. Do not attach the drawer face yet. Install the drawer in the table with drawer slides, inset ¾" (2cm) from the outside of the front of the Console Table (leaving room for the drawer face). Check that your drawer slides easily. When satisfied, position the drawer face on the drawer box so an even gap of approximately ⅛" (3mm) exists on all four sides. From the insides of the drawer, screw the drawer face on with 1¼" (3cm) screws for added support. Attach the drawer face with glue and 1¼" (3cm) finish nails. Repeat this process on the remaining drawer face. Install hardware.

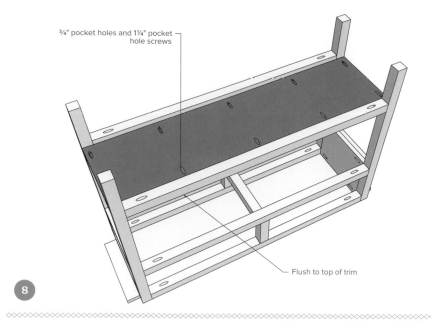

¾" pocket holes and 1¼" pocket hole screws

Flush to top of trim

8

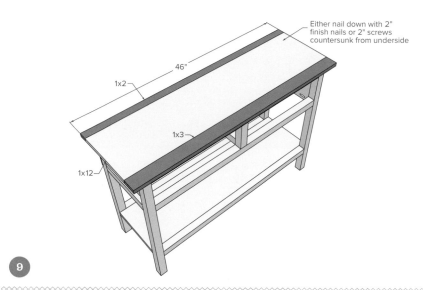

Either nail down with 2" finish nails or 2" screws countersunk from underside

46"

1x2

1x3

1x12

9

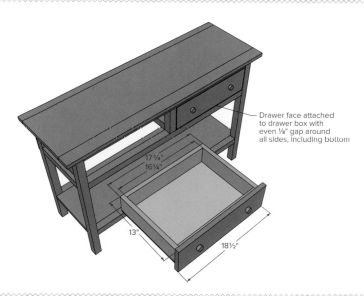

Drawer face attached to drawer box with even ⅛" gap around all sides, including bottom

17¾"
16¼"

13"

18½"

10

COMMON BUILDING MYTHS BUSTED

1 WOMEN DON'T DO WOODWORKING. The reality is, while most builders are men, woodworking is for anyone who wants to improve his *or her* home and lifestyle. With the tools available today, you do not need excessive strength to build furniture. Every day, I see more and more women picking up saws and nailers in the spirit of creating a better home on a budget. Woodworking is for everyone.

2 YOU NEED SPECIAL TOOLS TO BUILD FURNITURE. Yes, you will need a means to cut boards (if your hardware store does not make complimentary cuts), and yes, you will need a means to assemble furniture. But I have seen many projects built with the most basic of tools. Almost every project in this book can be made with a drill, a circular saw, and some hand tools.

Certainly, the more tools you have and the better your tools are, the easier it will be to build furniture. But you can—and many people do—build furniture with simple home improvement tools.

3 STORE-BOUGHT, FLAT-PACK FURNITURE IS INEXPENSIVE, SO WHY BOTHER MAKING YOUR OWN FURNITURE FROM SCRATCH? The funny thing is that if you buy flat-pack furniture, you have to partially build it anyway. You will most likely need basic tools and probably a drill. And most flat-pack furniture is made of particleboard, the lowest-quality, least-expensive wood available. Buying materials and making your own piece may be comparable to picking up a flat-pack bookcase at a big-box store. But when that bookcase falls apart in a year, is it really economical?

When you build your own furniture, you also have an extraordinary opportunity to build exactly what you need for your space and style. You can add an extra shelf or paint it a funky color. That odd nook nothing ever fits in? You can build furniture to fit it. Building your own furniture is definitely worth the bother!

4 USING POWER TOOLS IS DANGEROUS AND SCARY. Using power tools incorrectly is dangerous and scary, but using power tools correctly is not. Take time to learn how to use your power tools, and you will greatly lower any chance of injury.

5 YOU HAVE TO BE SET UP TO BUILD FURNITURE. You may not have a truck to haul boards. You may not have a garage or outdoor space to build furniture. But this does not mean you cannot. The old saying is true: Where there is a will, there is a way. Most home improvement stores will make free deliveries locally. In urban areas, workshops or studios are often part of community centers or community colleges. There are privately owned woodshops that you can rent by the hour. And I bet your dad would be pleasantly surprised if you showed up to borrow his garage and tools to build furniture for a weekend.

See if your home improvement store can make board cuts for you, leaving you just the assembly, which can be done in almost any space, even on your kitchen table.

For those of you who have ample space and tools, consider hosting woodworking parties for those who do not. Building is more fun with friends!

6 I DON'T HAVE TIME TO BUILD FURNITURE. When my daughter was an infant, I would wait for Grandma to show up and then sneak out the back door to work on furniture. Back then, I was grateful for just fifteen minutes to work on a project.

No one has extra time to build furniture. But you can make time. You can swap your workout for a carpentry session a few days a week. If you have small children, let them play with wood-block scraps while you build. Consider that by building furniture, you are saving money and improving the organization of your home, both of which will ultimately save you time.

4

THE

FAMILY
ROOM

LEFT: Gallery ledges • ABOVE RIGHT: LEGO
coffee table • BELOW: Rustic bench

A comfortable and well-organized

family room is essential for relaxing with your loved ones. In this chapter, I've included everything from a full media wall system for storing all your entertainment and media equipment to a coffee table that doubles as a play table, ledges for adding artwork or photos, and a bench to create extra seating or surfaces without sacrificing quality. You can also use the console table (page 40) from the entryway chapter as a sofa table or add the bedside table (page 141) in the bedroom chapter as an end table.

LEFT: Media tower · ABOVE RIGHT: Media console

GALLERY LEDGES

SHOPPING LIST

1x4: 2' per every foot of ledge

1x2: 1' per every foot of ledge

Wood glue

2" nails or screws *or* 1¼" pocket hole screws

3" screws or picture-hanging bracket

Finishing supplies

TOOLS

Basic hand tools

Finish nailer or pocket hole jig or drill with countersink bits

Stud finder (optional)

Level

CUTTING LIST

2 **1x4s** at desired ledge length

1 **1x2** at desired ledge length

IF YOU ARE ANYTHING LIKE ME, YOU like to accessorize your house. You want to change things up with the seasons by adding fresh photos and decor. But you want this change to be easy and fast. A simple gallery ledge allows you to keep your home updated season by season, holiday to holiday. Create a wall of vacation memories or use these customizable ledges to display collectibles. In just a few hours and for as many dollars, you can transform a blank wall into your favorite part of your home.

DIMENSIONS

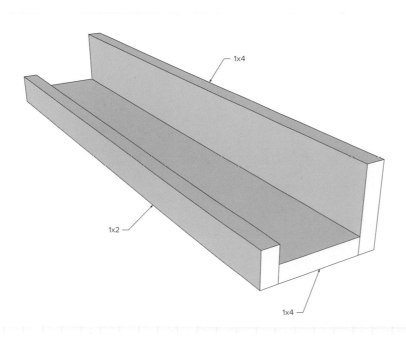

1x4

1x2

1x4

· BUILT BY ·
JAIME COSTIGLIO
www.thatsmyletter.blogspot.com

JAIME'S BEST DIY TRICKS:

1. Use what you have.

2. Build for your space, modify to fit.

3. Work in short intervals. Take small steps; I do this mostly out of necessity, but it aids in the thinking process, providing time to mull it over, and allows me to make better decisions.

4. If it doesn't exist, make it yourself.

5. Use simple tools: drill, saw, sander, sewing machine, nothing fancy.

❝ HOW I FINISHED THE LEDGES: I used scrap wood that had a lot of "character," primed and painted with two coats of off-white satin. I predrilled and countersank 2" wood screws through the back portion of the ledge and into the wall with mollys. ❞

1 BACK

If you are using pocket holes, drill ¾" pocket holes every 6" (15cm) to 8" (20.5cm) along both edges of the bottom of the shelf. Attach the back with glue and 1¼" (3cm) pocket hole screws.

Alternatively, for nails and countersunk screws, use ample glue and attach the bottom board to the back with 2" (5cm) screws or nails.

> ### NOTE
>
> Pocket holes will provide a stronger, better joint that's completely hidden on the underside. But if this is your first starter project and you do not own a pocket hole jig yet, you can attach with simple countersunk screws and glue.

2 FRONT

The front trim is both decorative and functional. It will keep your displays from falling off the narrow ledge. Attach it with either glue and 2" (5cm) finish nails or pocket hole screws if you drilled holes in the first step. Keep all edges flush to the bottom.

HANGING

To hang the ledges, locate the studs in your wall with a stud finder (optional) and mark them. Position the ledges on your wall, marking the location of studs on the back of the ledge. Predrill holes into the back of the gallery ledge, matching the stud location. Using 3" (7.5cm) screws through the predrilled holes, attach the back of the gallery ledge to the studs in the wall. Use a level to ensure your shelves are straight.

Alternatively, you can use a picture-hanging bracket to hang the shelves.

TIP If you hang more than one shelf, leave approximately 15" (38cm) between the two levels of shelves to allow for photos and other artwork.

PLANNING YOUR LEDGES

These ledges are simple to build, but you will want to plan out the length of your ledges to fit your wall space. Choosing lengths of 24" (61cm), 32" (81cm), 48" (122cm), and 96" (244cm) conserves the boards best. Lengths less than 24" (61cm) can present hanging challenges.

TIP Use painter's blue tape to mark out the location and length of your shelves on the wall. Adjust until you have found the perfect length. Build shelves to this length.

TIP Consider staggering shelves for added interest and to accommodate objects of varying heights.

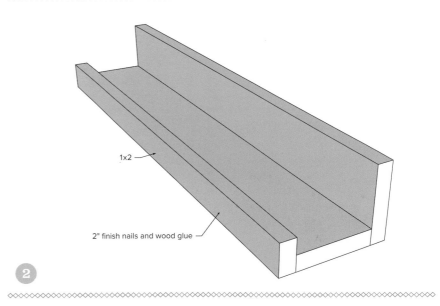

Attach back to bottom with 2" countersunk screws and glue

Pocket hole users can also attach bottom to back with ¾" pocket holes and 1¼" pocket hole screws

1

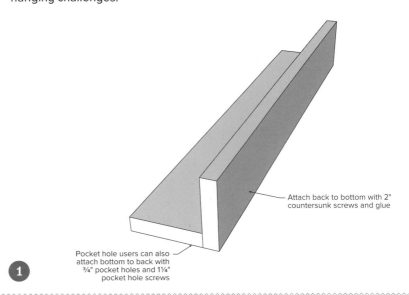

1x2

2" finish nails and wood glue

2

LEGO COFFEE TABLE

SHOPPING LIST

- ½ **sheet of ¾" MDF or hardwood plywood cut into strips 15⅞" wide x 48" long**
- 2   **8'-long 1x3s**
- 3   **8'-long 1x2s**
- 1   **12'-long 1x6**
- **Wood glue and filler**
- **1¼" screws**
- **2" screws**
- **1¼" pocket hole screws (optional)**
- **1¼" finish nails**
- **Knobs for false drawers (optional)**

TOOLS

- **Basic hand tools**
- **Drill**
- **Countersink drill bits**
- **Pocket hole jig (optional)**
- **Circular saw**
- **Finish nailer**
- **Level**

CUTTING LIST

- 2   **48"-long 1x6s** (side aprons)
- 3   **14⅜"-long 1x6s** (end aprons/divider)
- 2   **15⅞" x 48" pieces of ¾" MDF or plywood** (shelves)
- 4   **17¼"-long 1x2s** (end legs)
- 4   **17¼"-long 1x3s** (front/back legs)
- 2   **44½"-long 1x2s** (top supports)
- 2   **12⅞"-long 1x2s** (top supports, sides)
- 2   **48"-long 1x2s** (top sides)
- 2   **18⅞"-long 1x3s** (top ends)
- 2   **15⅞" x 24" pieces of ¾" MDF or plywood** (top inserts)

JUST BECAUSE YOU HAVE CHILDREN AND THEY like to play on your coffee table doesn't mean you have to sacrifice style. With this coffee table, you can have it all. This amazing table features removable top panels that lift out to reveal hidden storage. Use this hidden compartment to conceal toys, keep your laptop and files, or house favorite magazines. We've had this coffee table in our living room for a while now, and still love the simple design and hidden functionality.

1. BUILD THE BOX

Mark the placement of all joints on the sides, ends, and center and predrill the holes. Attach the ends and center to the box as shown. Use glue and 2" (5cm) screws or glue and 1¼" (3cm) pocket hole screws.

2. BOX BOTTOM

Attach one of the shelf pieces to the bottom of the box, using glue and 2" (5cm) screws.

3. END LEGS

Turn the project upside down and, using glue and 1¼" (3cm) screws, attach the end legs to the box. Keep legs flush to the outsides and top.

4. FRONT/BACK LEGS

Keeping the outside corners flush, attach front/back legs with glue and 1¼" (3cm) screws. Be very careful to create a perfect seam, giving the illusion of a solid leg.

Join legs together with 1¼" (3cm) finish nails.

5. BOTTOM SHELF

Attach the bottom shelf to the legs, 3" (7.5cm) from the bottom, with glue and 2" (5cm) screws. **Note:** If you plan on placing heavy items on the bottom shelf, it is a good idea to also add 1x2 trim to the edges of the shelf for additional reinforcement. Simply cut 1x2 boards to the lengths between the legs and attach with glue and 1¼" (3cm) finish nails.

6. TOP SUPPORTS

Use 1¼" (3cm) finish nails or screws to attach top supports all the way around the table. Carefully keep edges flush to the top.

7. TOP SIDES

Use glue and 2" (5cm) screws to attach the top sides to the top. If you have a pocket hole jig, you may wish to build the entire top first, prior to screwing it down.

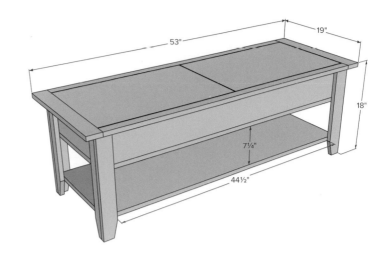

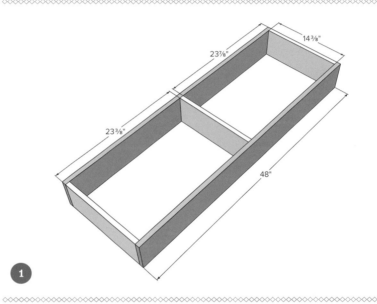

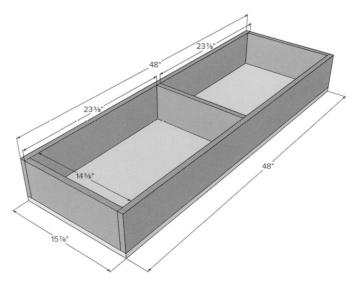

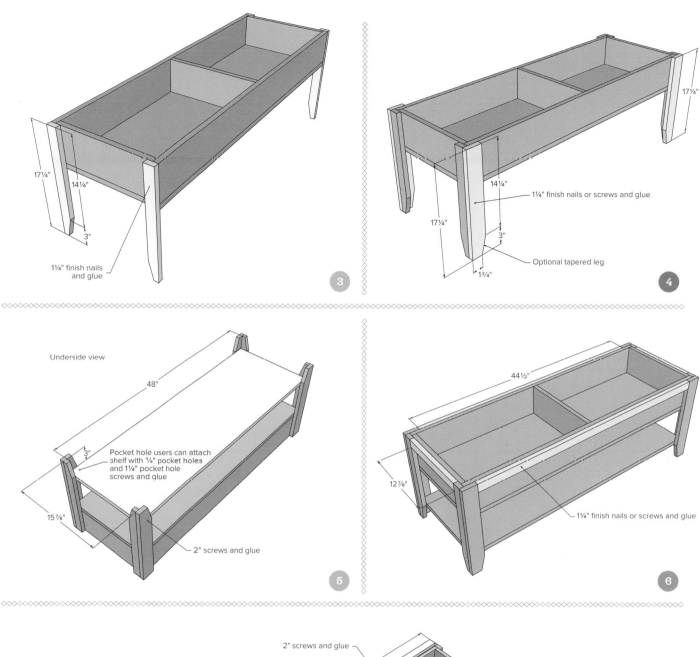

17¼"

14¼"

3"

1¼" finish nails
and glue

3

17¼"

14¼"

17¼"

3"

1¾"

1¼" finish nails or screws and glue

Optional tapered leg

4

Underside view

48"

3"

15⅞"

Pocket hole users can attach
shelf with ¾" pocket holes
and 1¼" pocket hole
screws and glue

2" screws and glue

5

44½"

12⅞"

1¼" finish nails or screws and glue

6

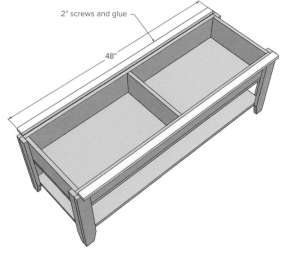

2" screws and glue

48"

7

8 TOP ENDS

Attach the top ends to the top of the project ends with glue and 2" (5cm) screws. Keep outside edges flush.

9 INSERTS

Fit inserts into the openings, checking to make sure they fit tightly but are easy to remove. If the inserts are not easy to remove, sand the edges and repeat until they are.

TIP You can drill a hole at least 3/4" wide in the inserts to use as a handle to pull up inserts.

Removable top panels disguise toy storage.

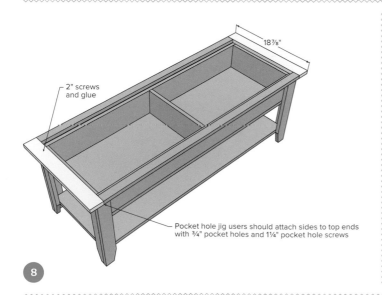

2" screws and glue

Pocket hole jig users should attach sides to top ends with ¾" pocket holes and 1¼" pocket hole screws

18⅞"

8

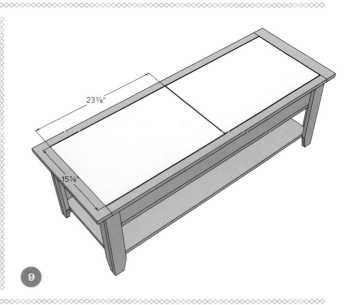

23⅞"

15⅞"

9

PROJECT
N° 6

MEDIA TOWER

THIS ATTRACTIVE TOWER CAN BE PAIRED with the media console (page 60) to make a full storage wall, or use it on its own as a bookcase anywhere in your home. The shelves are ideal for DVDs, books, or treasured collectibles.

SHOPPING LIST

- **3** 8'-long 1x2s
- **1** 6'-long 1x3
- **1** 8'-long 1x12
- **2** 12'-long 1x12s
- **1** sheet of ¼" plywood

Wood glue

2" finish nails (you can also use 1¼" pocket hole screws to build the box)

Shelf pins (for adjustable shelves, optional)

DOOR SHOPPING LIST (FOR 2 DOORS)

¼" plywood left over from cabinet

8' of hobby stock measuring ½" thick x 2½" wide (referred to as ½x3 boards)

1" pocket hole screws to build frame

⅝" brad nails to nail plywood to back of frame

- **2** sets of narrow butt mortise hinges
- **2** knobs or handles

Finishing supplies

TOOLS

Basic hand tools

Pocket hole jig

Drill with countersink drill bits (optional)

Finish nailer

Circular saw or other saw for making crosscuts

CUTTING LIST

- **6** 27"-long **1x12s** (shelves)
- **1** 30"-long **1x12** (top)
- **2** 71¼"-long **1x12s** (sides)
- **1** 28½" x 72" piece of ¼" plywood (back)
- **1** 28½"-long **1x3** (header)
- **2** 68¾"-long **1x2s** (side trim)
- **1** 25½"-long **1x2** (shelf trim)
- **1** 25½"-long **1x3** (base trim)
- **1** 30"-long **1x2** (top edge trim)

DOOR CUTTING LIST (FOR 2 DOORS)

- **4** 7½"-long **½x3s** (short door frame pieces)
- **4** 23¾"-long **½x3s** (long door frame pieces)
- **2** 12½" x 23¾" pieces ¼" plywood (door backs)

DIMENSIONS

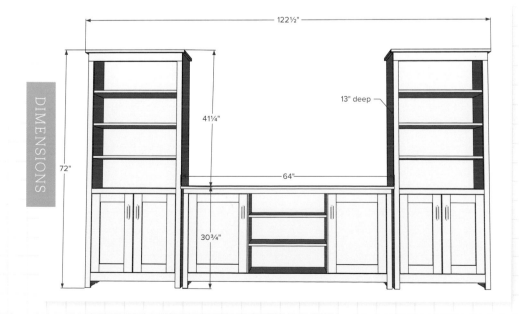

122½"

41¼"

13" deep

72"

64"

30¾"

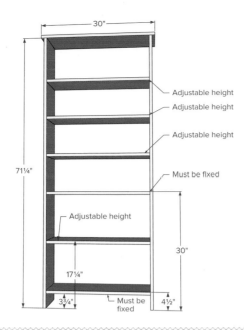

1

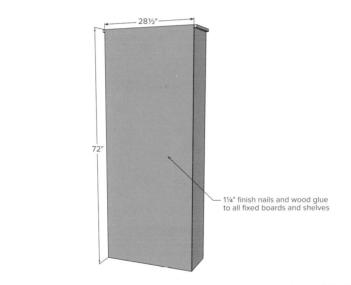

2

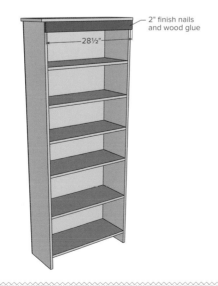

3

① BUILD THE BOX

Lay out the shelves according to measurements given in the diagram. The top, bottom, and center (29¼" [74.5cm] height) shelves must be fixed. All other shelves can be installed as floating with optional shelf pins, or they can also be fixed for added strength.

To attach fixed shelves, you can use a pocket hole jig set for ¾" (2cm) stock and 1¼" (3cm) pocket hole screws, or 2" (5cm) finish nails, or 2" (5cm) countersunk screws and glue.

The top overhangs the sides by ¾" (2cm). Tip: Use a scrap piece of 1x stock as a guide (1x stock is ¾" [2cm] thick).

② BACK

Apply glue to back edges on all fixed shelves. Lay the plywood back on, keeping edges flush with the project. Nail the back to all fixed shelves with 1¼" (3cm) finish nails. Tip: Use the first diagram to mark all shelf locations on the back to help you know where to nail.

③ HEADER

Apply glue to the back edges of the header board piece. Lay it on top of the project, top edge flush to the bottom edge of the top of the project. Ends are flush to the outside of the project. Attach with wood glue and 2" (5cm) finish nails.

4 SIDE TRIM

Apply glue to front edges of the sides and ¾" (2cm) in from the sides on all fixed shelves. Lay the side trim over the glued area, keeping outside edge flush. Nail down with 2" (5cm) finish nails, nailing to every fixed shelf for added support.

5 SHELF TRIM

Apply glue to the fixed center shelf and ends of the shelf trim. Lay on the shelf edge and nail down with 2" (5cm) finish nails. Also add two nails through the ends of the side trim for added support.

6 BASE TRIM

Apply glue to the bottom shelf and the ends of the base trim. Place the base trim over the glued areas. Nail on with 2" (5cm) nails. Also add two nails through the ends of side trim for added support.

7 TOP EDGE TRIM

Apply glue to the edge of the top and the top of the header. Place the top edge trim over the glued areas and nail on with 2" (5cm) nails. Nail from the face of the top edge trim to the front, and also from the top of top edge trim into the header below to secure the top edge trim from multiple directions for the greatest strength.

8 DOORS

Drill two ½" (13mm) pocket holes on both ends of each short door frame piece. Use 1" (2.5cm) pocket hole screws to build the door frames. Attach the back with glue and ⅝" (16mm) finish nails, ensuring doors are square and fit. Attach doors to cabinet using recommended narrow-profile butt hinges or other hinges. Install knobs or handles.

4   68¾"   Attach to fixed shelves with glue and 2" finish nails

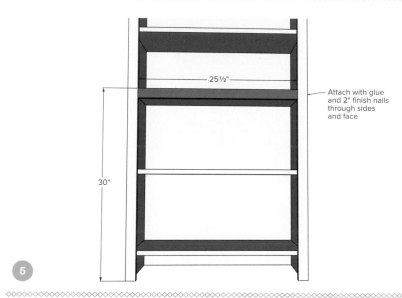

5   25½"   30"   Attach with glue and 2" finish nails through sides and face

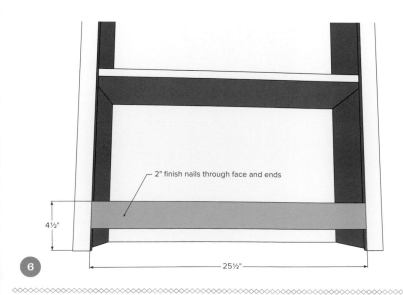

6   25½"   4½"   2" finish nails through face and ends

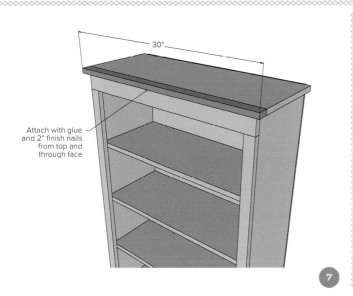

Attach with glue and 2" finish nails from top and through face

30"

7

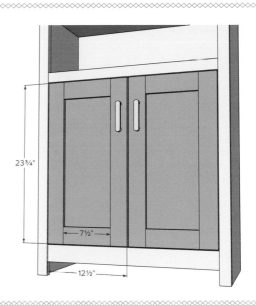

23¾"

7½"

12½"

8

· BUILT BY ·

HILLARY DICKMAN

http://thefriendlyhome.blogspot.com/

❝ My bookcases are backed with grass cloth reclaimed from old Roman shades. The wood is finished with flat black paint (no primer), lightly sanded and distressed, and then waxed with dark brown finishing wax. The wax lends the piece an incredibly smooth finish with a subtle sheen. ❞

MEDIA CONSOLE

AT 64" (163CM) WIDE, THIS MEDIA
console fits the largest flat-panel televisions. Doors help conceal less-attractive entertainment necessities, while the ample shelves hold controllers and gaming units. This functional media console will be an attractive addition to your hardworking family room. Pair it with two media towers (page 55) for a complete wall system.

DIMENSIONS

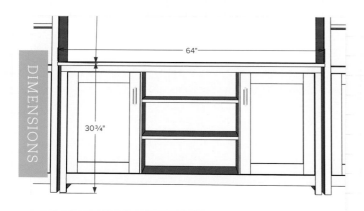

SHOPPING LIST

- 2 8'-long 1x12s
- 1 10'-long 1x12
- 2 8'-long 1x2s
- 1 6'-long 1x3
- 1 sheet of ¼" plywood
- 18' of hobby stock measuring ½" thick x 2½" wide (referred to as ½x3 boards)
- Wood glue
- 2" finish nails (you can also use 1¼" pocket hole screws to build the box)
- 2 sets of narrow butt mortise hinges
- 1" pocket hole screws to build frame
- ⅝" brad nails to nail plywood to back of frame
- 1¼" finish nails
- 2" finish nails
- 2 knobs/handles
- Shelf pins (for adjustable shelves, optional)

TOOLS

- Basic hand tools
- Pocket hole jig
- Finish nailer
- Circular saw
- Drill

CUTTING LIST

- 1 64"-long **1x12** (top)
- 1 61"-long **1x12** (bottom shelf)
- 2 30"-long **1x12s** (sides)
- 2 25½"-long **1x12s** (dividers)
- 2 23½"-long **1x12s** (shelves)
- 1 62½" x 30¾" piece of ¼" plywood (back)
- 1 62½"-long **1x2** (top trim)
- 1 64"-long **1x2** (top edge trim)
- 2 28½"-long **1x2s** (leg trim)
- 1 59½"-long **1x3** (base trim)
- 4 12½"-long **½x3s** (door frame)
- 4 23¾"-long **½x3s** (door frame)
- 2 17½" x 23¾" pieces of ¼" plywood (door backs)

· BUILT BY ·
HILLARY DICKMAN
http://thefriendlyhome.blogspot.com/

> This piece is the center of our home. It is visible from every public space in the house. It is big enough to fill a large space and accommodate a very large television, but shallow enough not to overwhelm the room.

HILLARY'S TIPS

- Because this is such a large piece, it is important to get each element square. Take your time putting it together.

- To make the shelves adjustable, it helps to use a shelving jig from a woodworking store. This jig (used to accurately drill shelf pinholes) will ensure that the holes for your shelf supports are evenly spaced and level.

- Make the whole unit sit flush with the wall by removing your baseboards and recutting them to butt up against the sides of the piece.

1 BUILD THE BOX

Carefully mark out all joints as shown in the diagram. If you are using a pocket hole jig, predrill all pocket holes for ¾" (2cm) stock. Starting on the inside, begin assembling the box. If you wish to keep the center shelves adjustable, you can attach them later using shelf pins and a shelf pin jig.

SHELF PIN JIG A shelf pin jig is a simple jig that you can use to accurately drill holes designed for use with shelf pins. Shelf pins enable you to have adjustable shelves in your projects.

The top overhangs each edge by ¾" (2cm).

TIP Use a 1x board as a guide to figure the overhang (1x boards are ¾" [2cm] thick).

2 BACK

Apply glue to all exposed edges on the back. Lay plywood on the back and nail down with 1¼" (3cm) finish nails. Make sure you mark out the location of all fixed boards on the plywood, and nail into those boards, as well.

3 TOP TRIM

Lay top trim in place and mark where it meets with the project. Remove the trim and apply glue within the marked areas. With the top trim flush to the bottom edge of the top piece, flush to the outsides, nail down with 2" (5cm) finish nails.

4 TOP EDGE TRIM

Apply glue to the edge of the top piece and the top edge of top trim. Place the top edge trim on the glue (outside edges are flush), and nail down from the top and front angles with 2" (5cm) nails.

5 LEG TRIM

Attach the leg trim to the console using wood glue and 2" (5cm) finish nails. Make sure you also attach it to the bottom shelf.

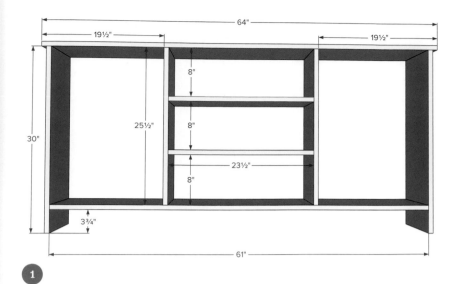

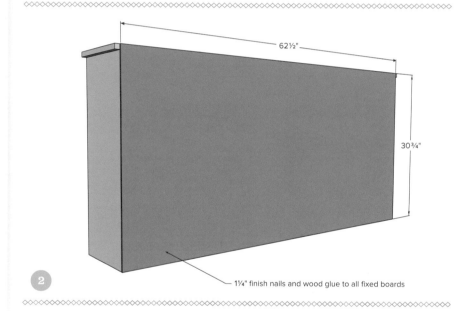

1¼" finish nails and wood glue to all fixed boards

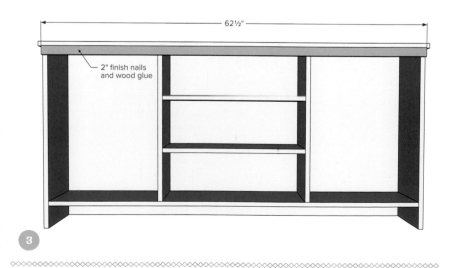

2" finish nails and wood glue

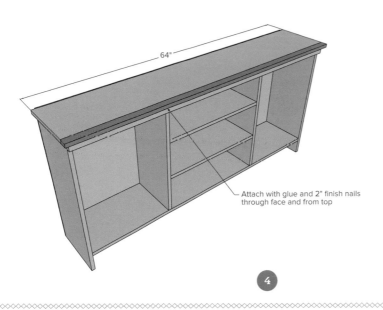

64"

Attach with glue and 2" finish nails through face and from top

④

⑥ BASE TRIM

Attach base trim to bottom shelf and dividers with glue and 2" (5cm) finish nails. Also use two nails on each end to secure leg trim to the bottom trim.

⑦ DOORS

Set the pocket hole jig for ½" (13mm) stock, and drill holes for the door frames. Construct the door frames. Attach plywood backs to door frames with wood glue and ⅝" (16mm) nails, securing well. Clamp and let dry on a flat surface. Attach doors to console with narrow-profile butt hinges following the manufacturer's instructions. Add hardware and catches to the doors to complete the project.

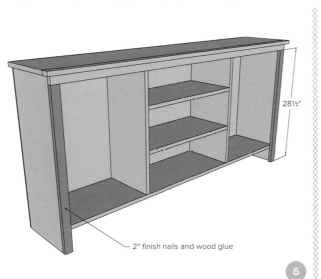

28½"

2" finish nails and wood glue

⑤

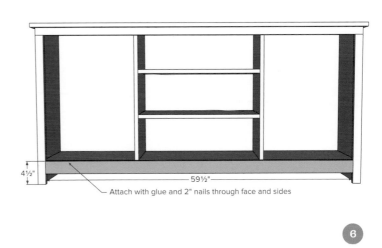

4½"

59½"

Attach with glue and 2" nails through face and sides

⑥

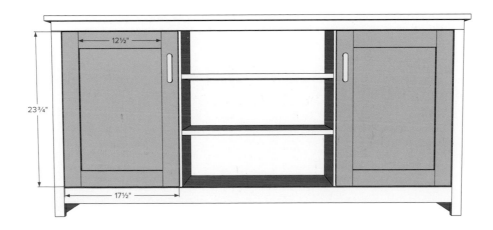

12½"

23¾"

17½"

⑦

rustic
BENCH

SHOPPING LIST

1   8'-long **1x8**

2   8'-long **1x3s**

2   8'-long **1x2s**

Wood glue

1¼" finish nails

2" finish nails

2" screws

Finishing supplies

TOOLS

Basic hand tools

Miter saw

Finish nailer

Drill with countersink bit

CUTTING LIST

4   17⅜"-long **1x3s**, both ends cut at 5 degrees off square, ends are parallel, measurement is short point to long point (legs)

2   39"-long **1x3s** (top side aprons)

2   39"-long **1x2s** (bottom supports)

2   11"-long **1x3s** (end aprons)

2   11"-long **1x2s** (bottom end supports)

2   41"-long **1x2s**, both ends cut at 18 degrees off square, ends are parallel, measurement is short point to long point (end/cross supports)

2   9½"-long **1x2s** (top supports)

2   47"-long **1x8s** (top)

WHETHER YOU USE THIS BENCH AS a coffee table for your family room or as occasional seating, the rustic design will add charming character to your space. This bench is surprisingly easy to make, and the cross-bracing adds support as well as interest. Use a miter saw to get your angles dead-on for best results.

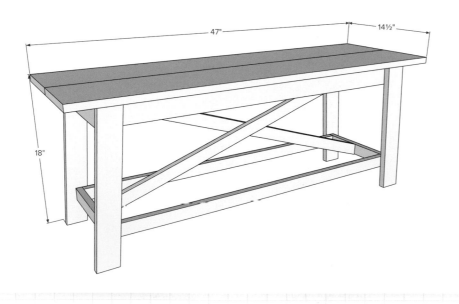

· BUILT BY ·

WHITNEY GAINER

shanty2chic, www.shanty-2-chic.com

"I am a stay-at-home mom to five kids. I have attempted (not always achieved) almost every craft. I've found along the way that I love the process of building my own treasures for our home. We recently finished building our home, and I have spent the last six months or so getting it dressed.

This project is super simple. It only took about forty-five minutes to build and can be used in just about any room in my home! I used two coats of latex paint and then distressed the edges a bit with stain to make it look even better."

1 MARK LEGS

Begin by marking the placement of the top side aprons on all four legs. Remember that two legs will be the same, two will be mirrored so your bench ends match. Measure carefully, and attach the top side aprons to the legs with wood glue and 1¼" (3cm) finish nails.

2 BOTTOM SUPPORT

Carefully measure and mark placement of bottom support, and attach to legs with wood glue and 1¼" (3cm) finish nails. You will need to build two sets of legs, as shown in the diagram.

3 END APRONS AND SUPPORTS

Once your leg sets are constructed, it is easy to join them to each other by attaching the end aprons and bottom end supports. This time, use glue and 2" (5cm) screws. This joint will take much abuse, so it is a good idea to use screws here.

4 END/CROSS SUPPORTS

Carefully cut your end/cross supports as directed in the cutting list. Mark the location of the cross supports on the end aprons and bottom end supports as shown in diagram, considering that the cross supports will sit on each side of the center of the end aprons and end supports.

Once you are satisfied with the placement, secure with wood glue and 2" (5cm) screws to the end aprons and a 1¼" finish nail where the cross supports overlap.

5 TOP SUPPORTS

We will need a little extra support at the top and something to nail the top piece to. Mark placement of the top supports and attach with wood glue and 2" (5cm) finish nails.

6 TOP

Rest the top boards on the base and attach with wood glue and 2" (5cm) finish nails, nailing them to all available boards.

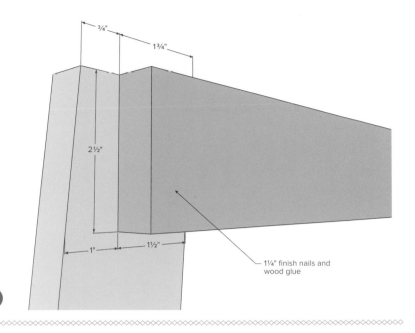

1¼" finish nails and wood glue

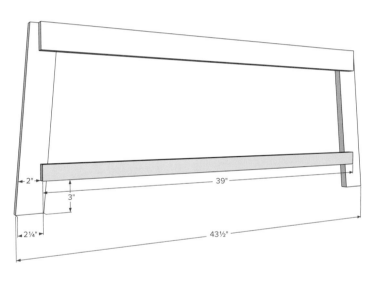

1x3

1x2

11"

2" screws and glue

Fasten from outside with screws and glue

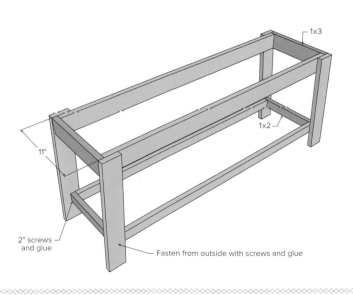

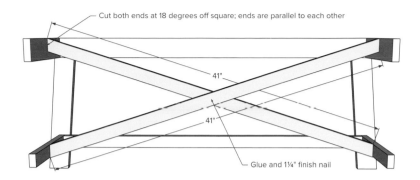

Cut both ends at 18 degrees off square; ends are parallel to each other

41"

41"

Glue and 1¼" finish nail

4

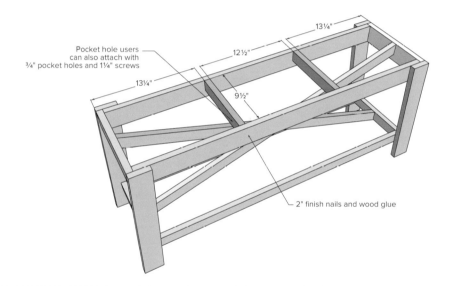

Pocket hole users can also attach with ¾" pocket holes and 1¼" screws

13¼"

12½"

13¼"

9½"

2" finish nails and wood glue

5

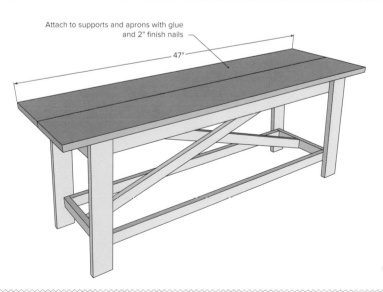

Attach to supports and aprons with glue and 2" finish nails

47"

· WHITNEY'S TIP ·

"I wouldn't scrimp on boards. I like to go with the premium pine when I can. It makes the building much easier."

6

5
THE
DINING ROOM

LEFT & BELOW: Hutch
ABOVE RIGHT: Farmhouse table

If the dining table is the heart of a

home, it should be warm and full of character, made of rich wood, and substantial enough for the home. For the dining room, you can build a farmhouse table and a matching bench to gather your family and friends around. And remember the console from the entryway? Simply add a hutch to create storage in the dining room. To economically and efficiently liven up wall space in your dining room, make simple wood frames from your scrap pile.

LEFT: Wall frames · ABOVE RIGHT: Farmhouse bench

WALL FRAMES

SHOPPING LIST

1	4'-long 1x3
1	6'-long 1x2
8	1¼" pocket hole screws
	1¼" finish nails
	Wood glue

TOOLS

Basic hand tools

Pocket hole jig

Circular saw or other saw for making crosscuts

Finish nailer

CUTTING LIST

2	14"-long **1x3s**
2	7"-long **1x3s**
2	12"-long **1x2s**
2	15½"-long **1x2s**

AS YOU BUILD PROJECTS IN THIS BOOK, YOU'LL find yourself building up quite a scrap pile! Save your scraps. I've included smaller projects that you can make for your home from these leftovers.

These photo frames are a more modern version of a barn-wood frame. They are the perfect size for standard 8" x 10" (20.5cm x 25.5cm) glass, or you can leave the frame open. Make it any size, add a corkboard or French ribbon board to the back—or even a mirror! This versatile frame can be used beyond the dining room!

DIMENSIONS

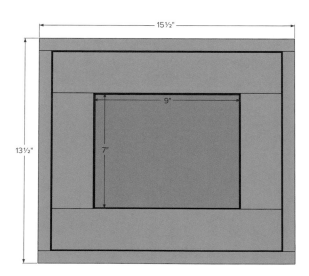

This frame accommodates 8" x 10" (20.5cm x 25.5cm) photos, but it can be modified for any size.

You can make these frames any size.

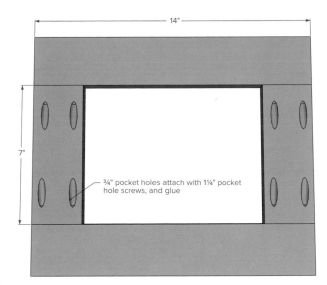

14"

7"

¾" pocket holes attach with 1¼" pocket
hole screws, and glue

1 INNER FRAME

Drill two ¾" (2cm) pocket holes on each
end of the shorter 1x3 boards. Attach
with 1¼" (3cm) pocket hole screws, and
glue to the longer 1x3 boards to create
a basic frame.

TIP Clamp the joint as you drive the screws
for a perfect joint.

2 OUTER FRAME ENDS

The inner frame is inset ¼" (6mm) on
the outer frame. The easiest way to do
this is to lay the inner frame on a scrap
piece of ¼"- (6mm-) thick plywood. The
plywood acts as a guide to raise your
inner frame ¼" (6mm) for attaching the
outer frame. Join the 1x2 outer frame
endboards to the inner frame with
wood glue and 1¼" (3cm) finish nails.
Discard scrap plywood.

3 OUTER FRAME SIDES

Attach the remaining 1x2 outer frame
pieces to the inner frame and outer
frame ends with wood glue and 1¼"
(3cm) finish nails.

4 GLASS OR OTHER BACKING

Glass can be attached with mirror clips
or permanently glued in place with
multisurface glue. Add your photos.
This frame is versatile and strong and
can be used for a variety of purposes
and applications.

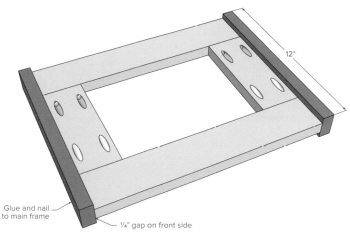

12"

Glue and nail
to main frame

¼" gap on front side

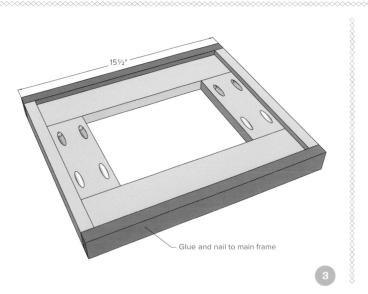

15½"

Glue and nail to main frame

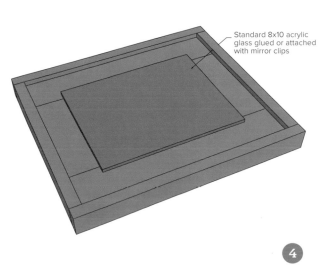

Standard 8x10 acrylic
glass glued or attached
with mirror clips

· BUILT BY ·
REBECCA RIDNER
BeccaDaleDesigns.com

" I want our house to be inviting and fun, so I fill it with bright colors, eclectic finds, and comfortable decor. Building furniture has opened up a whole new freedom in decorating and design. It still amazes me that a pile of lumber can turn into something beautiful that my family uses every day. I love that my children get to grow up in a house full of furniture their mother built.

I used 100-year-old wood to make the table. I love the character and history it adds. If you use reclaimed wood, I would invest in clamps and an electric plane. They will make your life so much easier. "

PROJECT
Nº 10

farmhouse
TABLE

THE ORIGINAL FARMHOUSE TABLES WERE simple, sturdy, and oversized. They were often built by the very people who would use them, with limited skills but lots of love. Farmhouse tables are traditionally oversized to seat family and farmworkers, and overbuilt to last forever.

Ours brings alive that same principle of building the furniture you really use. But I have updated the technique and styling to create a table that is easy to build and supersturdy, but not overly heavy. Paired with the farmhouse bench (page 76) or metal chairs, this farmhouse table takes on a new level of sophistication. It's kind of like a country gal in the city.

SHOPPING LIST

- 2 10'-long 1x4
- 4 10'-long 2x4s
- 2 8'-long 1x2s
- 3 8'-long 2x2s
- 7 8'-long 2x6s (or stud length)
- Wood glue
- 2" finish nails
- 2½" screws (pocket hole screws if you are using a pocket hole jig)
- 3" screws
- Finishing supplies

TOOLS

- Basic hand tools
- Finish nailer
- Drill with countersink bit
- Circular saw or other saw to make crosscuts
- Pocket hole jig (optional)

CUTTING LIST

- 4 37"-long **2x4s** (end apron/end support)
- 8 28½"-long **1x4s** (legs)
- 8 16¼"-long **1x2s** (leg spacers)
- 8 5¼"-long **1x2s** (short leg spacers)
- 2 60"-long **2x4s** (side aprons)
- 1 61½"-long **2x4** (stretcher)
- 7 31½"-long **2x2s** (under-table supports)
- 7 78"-long **2x6s** (tabletop boards)

DIMENSIONS

78" 38½" 30"

NOTES

- Use boards with square edges, especially the 1x2 spacers, to create the illusion of a solid leg.

- On the legs, line the edges up to give the legs the illusion of a solid piece of wood.

- Any exposed screw holes in the top of the table should be placed in a pattern.

- Check for square after each step and use glue.

- Minimize the gaps between the tabletop boards; if you have a pocket hole jig, build your tabletop first, then attach it.

1 LEG ENDS

Mark each end apron and end support ½" (13mm) from the outer edge. Test to make sure the legs fit by dry-fitting the legs over the end aprons, marking their placement. Remove and apply glue within the marks. Fit the legs on the aprons and nail down with 2" (5cm) finish nails, making sure the legs are square. You will need to build two sets of legs.

2 LEG SPACERS

Apply glue to one edge of the leg spacers. Nail each leg spacer in place with 2" (5cm) finish nails. Keep the outsides flush, creating the illusion of a solid leg. Add spacers to both leg sets.

3 SIDE APRONS/LEGS

Apply glue to the end of the side aprons and screw on remaining leg pieces. Tip: Use a scrap piece of 1x board as a spacer; it's ¾" (2cm) thick and works perfectly as a guide.

4 TABLE FRAME

Apply glue on all inside edges of the leg sets. Nail the side apron pieces to the leg sets with 2" (5cm) finish nails, spaced every 6" (15cm) to 8" (20.5cm).

5 STRETCHER

Mark placement of stretcher on base end supports. Apply glue to ends of the stretcher and screw the stretcher in place with 3" (7.5cm) screws.

6 UNDER-TABLE SUPPORTS

Attach under-table supports to side aprons with either 3" screws or 2½" pocket hole screws, spaced as shown in diagram, flush to top of table.

TIP Cut a scrap board 6" long and use it as a spacer between 6" long measurements to save time.

7 TABLETOP BOARDS

If you have a pocket hole jig, you can build the tabletop first with 1½" (3.8cm) pocket holes and 2½" (6.5cm) pocket hole screws. Otherwise, attach the tabletop boards, starting in the center and working your way outward, with glue and 2½" (6.5cm) screws. Minimize the gaps between the boards as you go by placing boards as close as possible as you screw down.

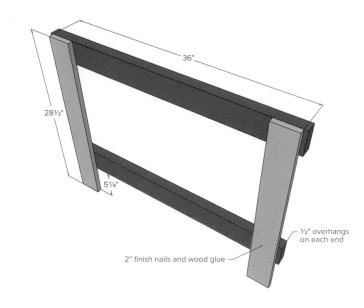

36"

28½"

5¼"

½" overhangs on each end

2" finish nails and wood glue

1

16¼"

2" finish nails and glue

5¼"

2

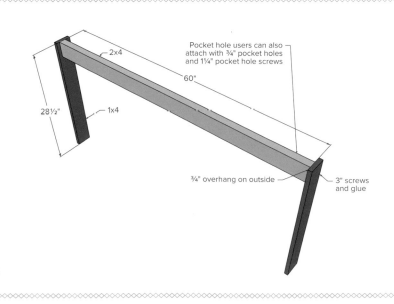

Pocket hole users can also attach with ¾" pocket holes and 1¼" pocket hole screws

2x4

60"

28½"

1x4

¾" overhang on outside

3" screws and glue

3

The stretcher can be placed on top of the end supports for a different look. Add 4" (10cm) to the stretcher length, and overhang the ends by ½" (13mm). Use 3" (7.5cm) screws centered on the end supports to fasten the stretcher down.

2" nails and glue

4

61½"

13¾"

13¾"

5

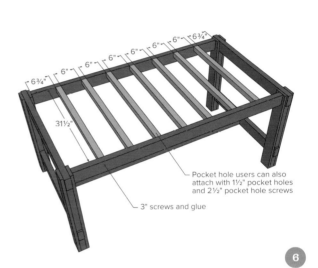

6¾" 6" 6" 6" 6" 6" 6¾"

6¾" 6" 6"

31½"

Pocket hole users can also attach with 1½" pocket holes and 2½" pocket hole screws

3" screws and glue

6

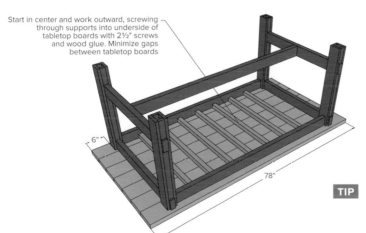

Start in center and work outward, screwing through supports into underside of tabletop boards with 2½" screws and wood glue. Minimize gaps between tabletop boards

6"

78"

7

farmhouse
BENCH

SHOPPING LIST

2   8'-long 1x12s

2   8'-long 1x2s

2   8'-long 1x3s

Wood glue

2" finish nails

Finishing supplies

TOOLS

Basic hand tools

Jigsaw

Circular saw

Finish nailer

CUTTING LIST

2   17¼"-long **1x12s** (sides)

1   52"-long **1x12** (bottom shelf)

1   59½"-long **1x12** (bench top)

2   59½"-long **1x3s** (top trim)

2   15½"-long **1x2s** (side trim)

1   50½"-long **1x2** (bottom shelf trim)

A SIMPLE WOOD BENCH WITH A FEW
pretty details will bring character and charm to any space. With this farmhouse bench, we've created economical and attractive seating for our farmhouse table (page 73). But this bench could also work at the foot of a bed, as a spot to sit and remove boots in the entryway, or even as a coffee table. It is simple to build, yet sturdy and strong, and it makes the perfect beginner project. The only power tools you must have are a jigsaw and a finish nailer.

DIMENSIONS

The farmhouse bench measures 59½" wide by 13" deep by 18" tall (151cm x 33cm x 45.5cm). It is designed to seat three adults and is standard seating height.

· BUILT BY ·

REBECCA RIDNER

BeccaDaleDesigns.com

M28-7
STORAGE BARREL
CAP 59 GAL

1 CUTTING ENDS

A few pretty details can add considerable charm to a basic bench. Mark the boards cut for the sides as shown in the diagram, and carefully cut them out with a jigsaw. Sand the edges until smooth.

2 BOTTOM SHELF

On both of the sides, measure 4" (10cm) up from the bottom and mark. Use your speed square to draw a line. Attach the bottom shelf to the sides with wood glue and 2" (5cm) finish nails, using the line as a guide, even with the bottom of the shelf. Use glue on all joints.

3 BENCH TOP

Mark the underside of the bench top 3" (7.5cm) from the outside edge on both ends. Apply wood glue to the tops of the legs. Position the bench top on the legs, matching marks for overhangs. Nail the bench top to the legs with 2" (5cm) finish nails.

4 TOP TRIM ENDS

Using the diagram to guide you, create a pattern for the ends of the top trim. Cut out with a jigsaw, and use this pattern to cut decorative ends on the bench side top trim. After cutting, sand the edges until smooth.

5 ATTACHING TOP TRIM

Apply glue to the edge of the top and 2" (5cm) down the legs. With tops and ends flush, nail the top trim to the sides of the bench with 2" (5cm) nails.

6 SIDE TRIM

Apply glue to the exposed edges of legs and ¾" (2cm) in on the bottom shelf. Nail the leg trim to the legs with 2" (5cm) nails, keeping outside edges flush. Also nail the trim to the bottom shelf for increased strength and support.

7 BOTTOM SHELF TRIM

Check to make sure the bottom shelf trim fits well, trimming if necessary. Remove and apply glue along edge of bottom shelf. With top edges flush, attach bottom shelf trim to bottom shelf with 2" (5cm) nails. Add two nails per end through the outside of the leg trim into the end grain of the bottom shelf trim.

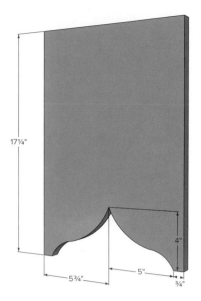

1

17¼"

4"

5¾"   5"   ¾"

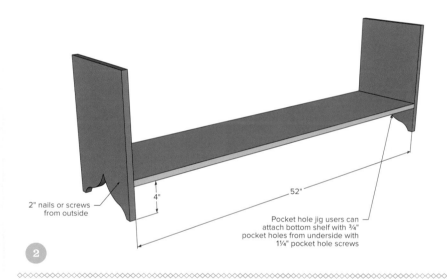

Fasten top to sides with 2" finish nails

59½"

Pocket hole jig users can also attach sides to top with ¾" pocket holes and 1¼" pocket hole screws

3

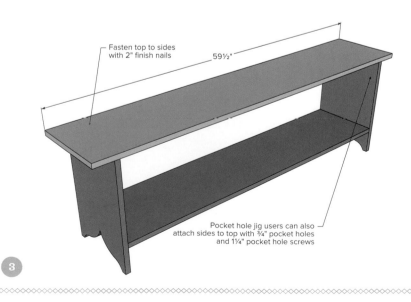

2" nails or screws from outside

4"

52"

Pocket hole jig users can attach bottom shelf with ¾" pocket holes from underside with 1¼" pocket hole screws

2

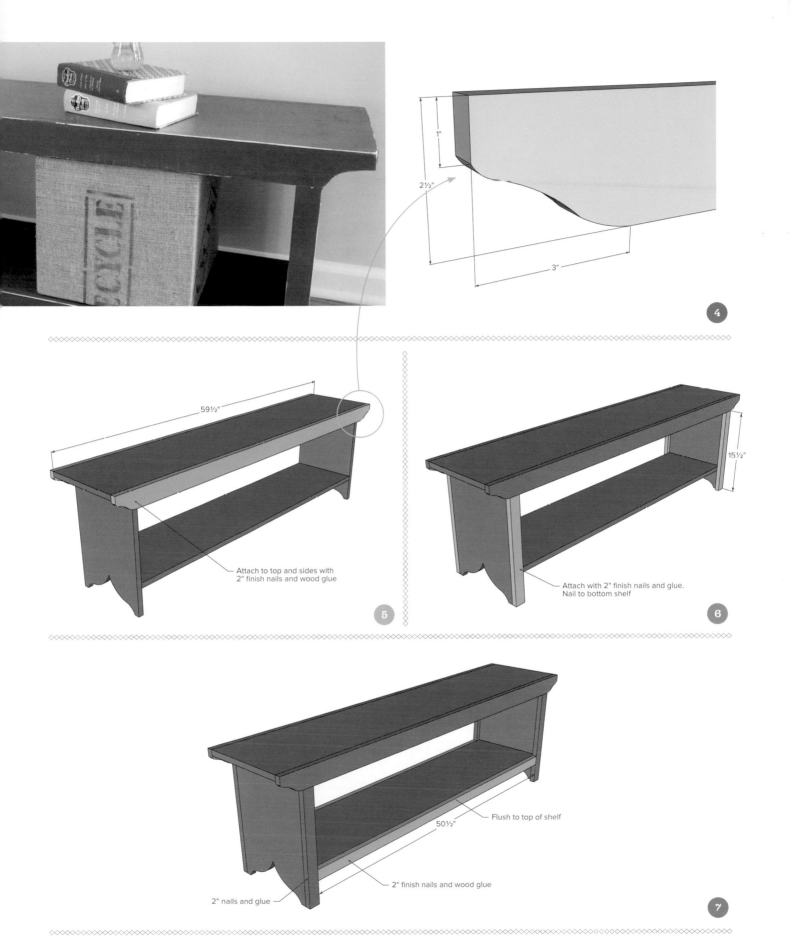

1"

2½"

3"

4

59½"

Attach to top and sides with
2" finish nails and wood glue

5

15½"

Attach with 2" finish nails and glue.
Nail to bottom shelf

6

Flush to top of shelf

50½"

2" finish nails and wood glue

2" nails and glue

7

· BUILT BY ·
ASHLEY MILLS
thehandmadehome.net

HUTCH

I LOVE HUTCHES. THEY ARE SO EASY
to make, yet they add so many possibilities
for storage and display. This hutch is
designed to work with the console table
(page 40). Use it to display serving trays and
dishes, or any favorite decorative objects.
This hutch is surprisingly easy to make. It's
really just a bookcase with no bottom.

SHOPPING LIST

1 8'-long 1x2
1 4'-long 1x3
1 4'-long 1x6
2 8'-long 1x12s
1 4'-long 1x12
½ sheet of ¼" plywood
1 8'-long ¾" x ¾" molding
   for top crown
Wood glue
1¼" pocket hole screws
(if using a pocket hole jig,
optional)
1¼" finish nails
2" finish nails
Finishing supplies

TOOLS

Basic hand tools
Finish nailer
Pocket hole jig (optional)
Jigsaw
Sander and sandpaper
Miter saw

CUTTING LIST

1 45½"-long **1x12** (top)
2 42"-long **1x12s** (sides)
2 40½"-long **1x12s** (shelves)
1 42" x 42¾" piece of ¼"
   plywood (back)
2 36½"-long **1x2s** (side trim)
1 42"-long **1x6** (header)
1 45½"-long **1x3** (top front)
Crown molding cut to fit

(page 40)

DIMENSIONS

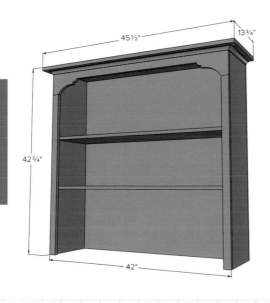

45½"   13¾"

42¾"

42"

1 BUILD THE BOX

Measure and mark the top board 1¾" (4.5cm) from each end. This is the overhang on top. Measure and mark the location of the shelves on the sides. Build the box using either glue and 2" (5cm) finish nails or ¾" (2cm) pocket holes and 1¼" (3cm) pocket hole screws.

2 BACK

Apply glue to edges of back, except for the overhangs on top. With project facedown, lay the plywood back on. Nail on with 1¼" (3cm) nails. Mark the location of shelves from step 1 on this plywood back and nail it to the fixed shelves as well for added support.

3 SIDE TRIM

Turn the hutch over so it is face up. Lay side trim on the hutch sides as shown in the diagram and mark the location of the side trim. Remove and apply glue to exposed edges within the marked area on sides of hutch. Lay side trim on top of the glue and nail down with 2" (5cm) nails. Keep bottom edges flush. Also add nails to all fixed shelves to further reinforce shelf strength.

4 HEADER

Mark the decorative pattern on the header as directed in diagram. Use a jigsaw to carefully cut the pattern out. Once finished, sand the edges of the header until smooth and even. Apply glue to the top exposed portions of the side edges. Lay the header in place and nail down with 2" (5cm) nails.

5 FRONT EDGE TRIM

Apply glue to the top edge of the header and the front edge of the top. Set the front edge trim in place and nail down with 2" (5cm) nails. We will be further supporting this joint with crown molding in the next step, so do not worry.

6 MOLDING

Cut the top crown molding, mitering ends to fit the underside of the top. Glue and secure with 1¼" (3cm) nails.

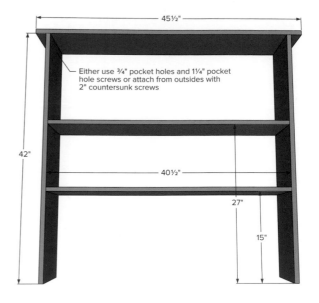

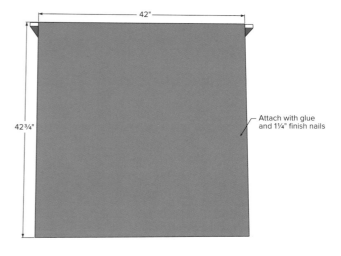

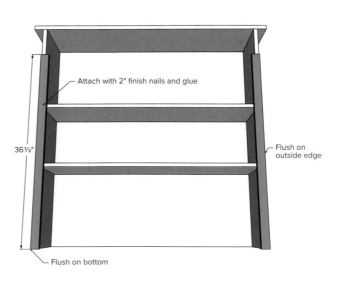

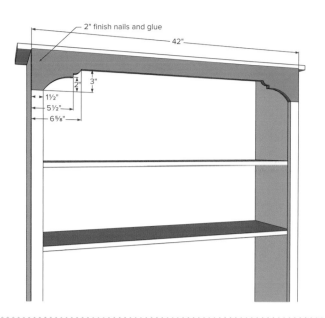

2" finish nails and glue

42"

3"
½"
1½"
5½"
6⅝"

4

Hutches must always be secured to a stud in the wall to keep the hutch from tipping forward. Invest in a tip-resistant kit for added safety. Also attach to console.

2" finish nails and wood glue

45½"

5

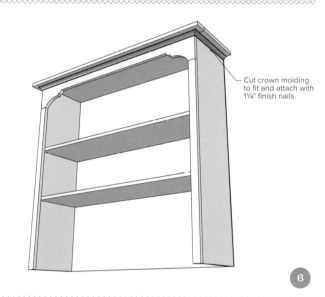

Cut crown molding to fit and attach with 1¼" finish nails

6

6

KITCHEN & BATH

LEFT & BELOW: Recycling console
ABOVE RIGHT: Step stool

Add a little touch of handmade to

your kitchen and bathrooms with projects ranging from a versatile kitchen island, a recycling console featuring a tilt-out trash bin, or a vintage-style step stool, to functional and attractive bathroom wall storage. You can use these projects in other rooms as well. The kitchen island makes a great craft table, and the recycling console can be used as a laundry hamper. The step stool will work in a child's room, and the wall storage can provide a little extra stylish organization anywhere.

LEFT: Kitchen island · ABOVE RIGHT: Bathroom wall storage

PROJECT N° 13

RECYCLING CONSOLE

MAKE RECYCLING A SEAMLESS PART OF your family's life with a dedicated recycling center. This recycling center features a foldout trash compartment and three shelves. Keep bags, cans, or glass in the shelves, and place unsightly trash out of sight in the foldout compartment. The top of this recycling center offers ample space for use as a work surface or additional storage.

SHOPPING LIST

- **3** 8'-long **1x12s**
- **1** 8'-long **1x2**
- **2** 8'-long **1x3**
- **½** sheet of ¼" plywood
- Wood glue
- Either 2" screws or 1¼" pocket hole screws
- ¾" finish nails
- 1¼" finish nails
- 2" finish nails
- Shelf pins (for adjustable shelves, optional)
- **1** set of narrow-profile butt hinges
- **1** magnetic clasp
- **1** small chain
- Knob or handle (for foldout compartment door)
- Finishing supplies

TOOLS

- Basic hand tools
- Pocket hole jig
- Circular saw or other saw for making crosscuts
- Finish nailer
- Drill and countersink bit (optional)
- Jigsaw

CUTTING LIST

- **1** 32"-long **1x12** (top)
- **1** 28½"-long **1x12** (bottom shelf)
- **2** 29¼"-long **1x12s** (sides)
- **1** 26¾"-long **1x12** (center divider)
- **2** 13¾"-long **1x12s** (shelves)
- **1** 32" x 30" piece of ¼" plywood (back)
- **2** 32"-long **1x2s** (header)
- **1** 32"-long **1x3** (footer)
- **1** 25¼"-long **1x2** (side trim)
- **2** 17½"-long **1x3s** (door frame)
- **2** 20"-long **1x3s** (door frame)
- **2** 11½"-long **1x12s**, longest point measurement, one end cut at 45 degrees (foldout compartment sides)
- **1** 14¼"-long **1x12** (foldout compartment bottom)
- **1** 14¼" x 22¾" piece of ¼" plywood (foldout door back)

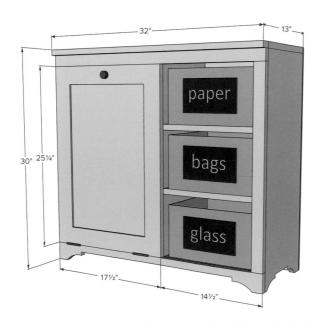

DIMENSIONS

The tilt-out compartment hides recycling.

1 BUILD THE BOX

Mark placement of all joints on top, bottom, and sides. If you are using pocket holes, drill all pocket holes prior to assembly. Apply glue to both ends of divider and attach to top and bottom as marked. Use either 1¼" (3cm) pocket hole screws or 2" (5cm) countersunk screws or finish nails.

Once the center divider is in place, add the sides to the project.

2 SHELVES

Measure and mark the placement of the small shelves inside the shelf compartment. Apply glue to the edges of the shelves and insert them. Use 2" (5cm) nails to fasten the shelves in place.

3 BACK

Turn the project on its face, back side up. Consult the diagrams for shelf placement and mark them on the back. Apply glue to all exposed back edges. Lay the plywood back on and nail it down with 1¼" (3cm) finish nails. You also will want to nail into any fixed shelves for added strength.

4 HEADER

Turn the project back over on its back. Lay the header on the top of the project, with the top edge of the header flush to the bottom edge of the top. Mark its placement, and set the header aside. Apply glue within marked areas. Replace the header, and nail on with 2" (5cm) nails.

5 FOOTER

Apply glue on the lower 2" (5cm) of the front of the sides of the project and along the exposed edge of the bottom shelf. Place the footer over the glued area, with edges flush to outsides, bottom shelf, and bottom of project. Nail on with 2" (5cm) nails.

6 SIDE TRIM

Place side trim on top side of project. Mark the placement on all box boards, and remove the side trim. Apply glue within the marked area, and replace side trim. With outside edges flush, nail the side trim to the side and shelves of the project.

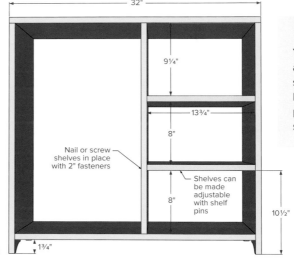

Can be attached with glue and 2" countersunk screws
32"
Optional ¾" pocket holes and 1¼" pocket hole screws
29¼"
26¾"
1¾"
16¾"
14½"

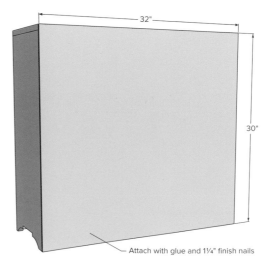

32"
9¼"
13¾"
8"
Nail or screw shelves in place with 2" fasteners
Shelves can be made adjustable with shelf pins
8"
10½"
1¾"

NOTE

You can alternatively leave shelves out and later add with shelf pins for adjustable shelves.

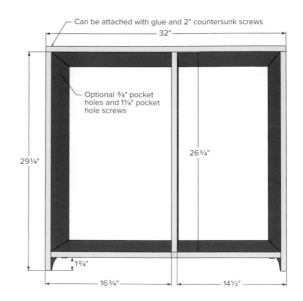

32"
30"
Attach with glue and 1¼" finish nails

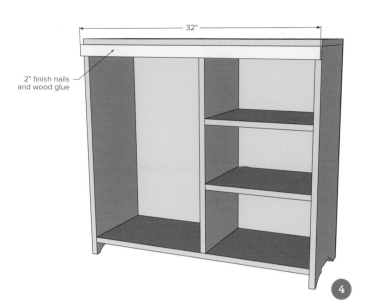

2" finish nails and wood glue

4

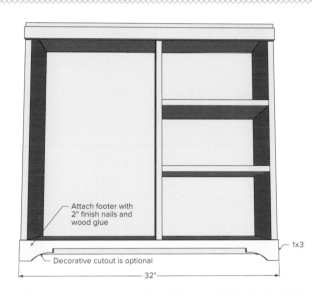

Attach footer with 2" finish nails and wood glue

Decorative cutout is optional

1x3

32"

5

NOTE

An optional decorative pattern can be cut out of the footer with a jigsaw.

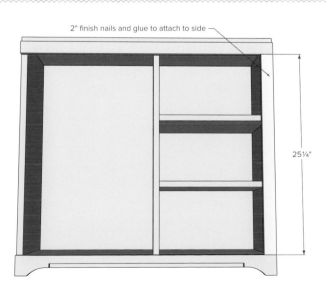

2" finish nails and glue to attach to side

25¼"

6

7 TABLETOP EDGE

Apply glue on top of header and on front edge of tabletop. Place the tabletop edge piece on the header, held flush to both the tabletop and ends. Nail through the face into the tabletop front edge with 2" (5cm) nails. Then nail through the top into the header with 2" (5cm) nails.

8 DOOR FRAME

Build the door frame using 1x3 boards. Use a pocket hole jig set for ¾" (2cm) stock, two pocket holes per end per side of door frame. Use wood glue and 1¼" (3cm) pocket hole screws.

9 FOLDOUT COMPARTMENT

With the frame built, build the tilt-out compartment with 1x12s as shown in diagram (either with pocket holes or 2" [5cm] screws) and then attach to the door frame as shown in diagram, leaving a ⅞" (2.2cm) gap on either side of the door frame, flush to bottom.

10 DOOR FRAME BACK

Dry-fit the plywood in the foldout door. Trace the outline of the plywood and remove it. Apply glue within the traced outline. Replace the plywood and nail on with 1" (2.5cm) nails.

11 HINGES

Position the door inside the opening and use narrow-profile butt mortise hinges to attach it. A magnetic clasp will prevent the door from falling open. Installing a chain will keep the door from opening too wide. Install knob or handle.

12 DECORATIVE BASE

For a softer, more country feel, use a jigsaw to cut out a pattern in the footers and, if desired, the sides.

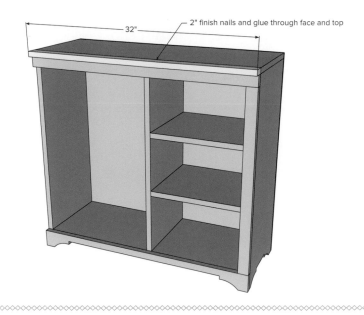

32"

2" finish nails and glue through face and top

7

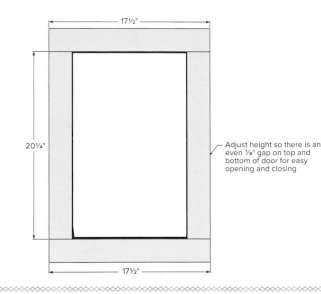

17½"

20¼"

17½"

Adjust height so there is an even ⅛" gap on top and bottom of door for easy opening and closing

8

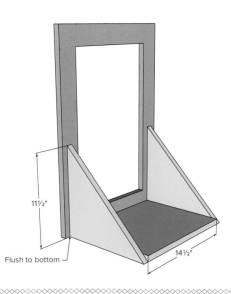

11½"

14½"

Flush to bottom

9

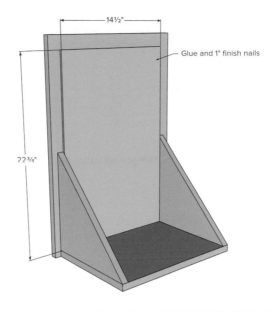

14½"

22¾"

Glue and 1" finish nails

10

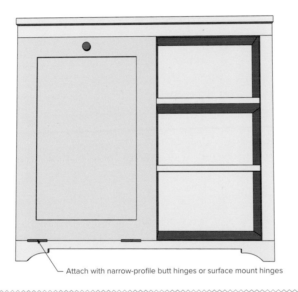

NOTE

Door can be installed on either side of console.

Attach with narrow-profile butt hinges or surface mount hinges

11

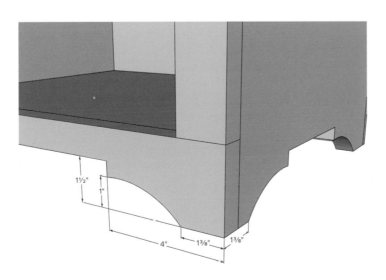

1½"

1"

4"   1⅜"   1⅜"

12

This stool is so sturdy, I use it for reaching
the top shelf.

STEP STOOL

I MADE A STEP STOOL YEARS AGO
with all the charm and cuteness of a vintage find, but I didn't share the plans due to the complicated cuts. After much thought, I found a way to simplify the construction of this stool, so anyone can build it for their home.

SHOPPING LIST

- 1   3'-long 1x12
- 1   8'-long 1x2
- 1   3'-long 1x8
- Wood glue
- Either 2" screws or 1¼" pocket hole screws

TOOLS

- Basic hand tools
- Jigsaw
- Power sander and sandpaper
- Miter saw capable of making bevel cuts
- Pocket hole jig
- Drill with countersink drill bit

CUTTING LIST

- 2   15½"-long **1x12s** (sides)
- 2   12½"-long **1x2s**, short point to short point, both ends angled at 10 degrees off square, ends *not* parallel (top supports)
- 3   14¾"-long **1x2s**, short point to short point, both ends angled at 10 degrees off square, ends *not* parallel (base supports)
- 1   14⅜"-long **1x8**, short point to short point, both ends beveled at 10 degrees off square, ends *not* parallel (bottom step)
- 1   15"-long **1x8** (top step)

DIMENSIONS

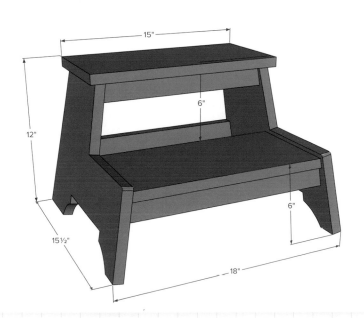

1 SIDE PATTERNS

On the side pieces, carefully measure and mark out the pattern using the measurement points given. With a jigsaw, cut out the sides. Round the edges and smooth and soften cuts with a sander, making sure both cuts match.

2 TOP ANGLE

With your miter saw, circular saw, or jigsaw set at 10 degrees off square, bevel the top edge of the sides.

3 TOP SUPPORTS

Either drill ¾" (2cm) pocket holes on each end of top supports and attach with 1¼" (3cm) pocket hole screws or attach top supports with glue and 2" (5cm) screws, flush to the top.

4 BASE SUPPORTS

Mark the location of base supports on inside of sides, and attach with either ¾" (2cm) pocket holes and 1¼" (3cm) pocket hole screws or 2" (5cm) countersunk screws. Your stool should sit level.

5 BOTTOM STEP

Dry-fit the bottom step in the stool. Remove and apply glue to tops of the base supports and end of the bottom step. Replace the bottom step and screw down to base supports with 2" (5cm) screws and glue. Also screw from the sides for added support.

6 TOP STEP

Dry-fit the top step on the stool. Remove and apply glue to all exposed edges. Replace the top and screw down with a countersink bit and 2" (5cm) screws.

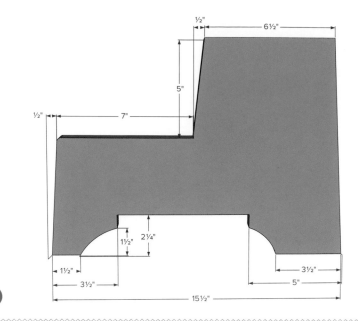

1

½"   6½"   ½"
5"
7"
2¼"
1½"
1½"   3½"   3½"   5"
15½"

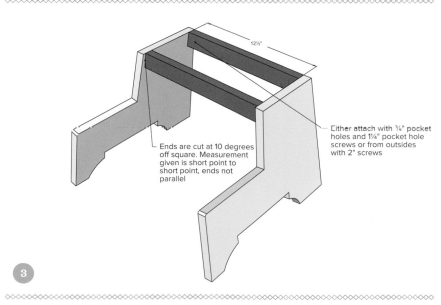

Bevel this top edge at 10 degrees off square, keeping longest point on the inside. Both sides will need to be beveled in mirror to create two sides

11¼"

Round front corner

2

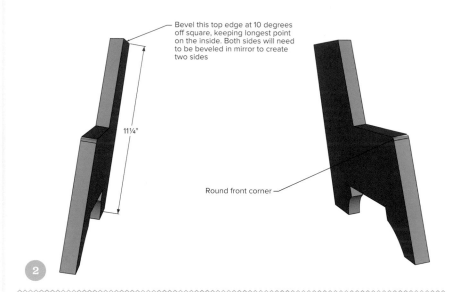

12½"

Either attach with ¾" pocket holes and 1¼" pocket hole screws or from outsides with 2" screws

Ends are cut at 10 degrees off square. Measurement given is short point to short point, ends not parallel

3

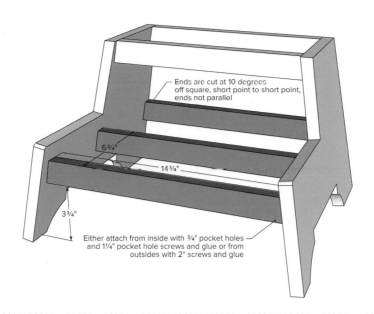

Ends are cut at 10 degrees off square, short point to short point, ends not parallel

6¾"

14¾"

3¾"

Either attach from inside with ¾" pocket holes and 1¼" pocket hole screws and glue or from outsides with 2" screws and glue

4

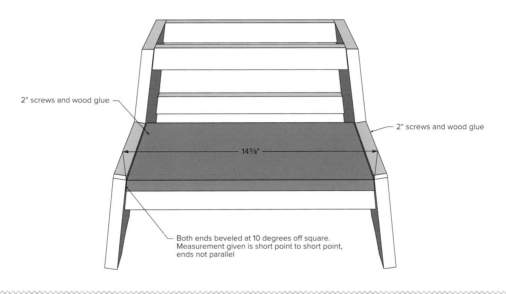

2" screws and wood glue

2" screws and wood glue

14⅜"

Both ends beveled at 10 degrees off square. Measurement given is short point to short point, ends not parallel

5

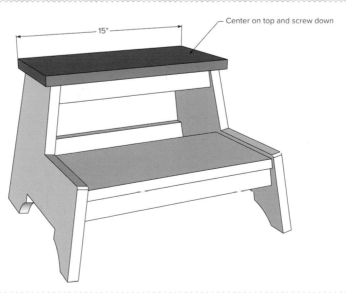

15"

Center on top and screw down

6

PROJECT
Nº 15

bathroom
WALL
STORAGE

WITH LITTLE SHELVES AND CUBBIES,
this bathroom wall storage unit is the perfect spot for storing everything from pretty soaps to neatly folded towels. Shelves can be made adjustable to accommodate taller items. This also has an optional open back so your wall color can peek through. To hang it securely, attach directly to a stud in the wall.

SHOPPING LIST

- **1** 8'-long 1x2
- **2** 8'-long 1x10
- **¼** sheet of ¼" plywood
- **1** 8'-long stick molding, ¾" x ¾"

Wood glue

1¼" pocket hole screws or 2" screws

2" finish nails

1¼" finish nails

16 shelf pins

3" screws for hanging into wall or heavy-duty hanging kit

TOOLS

Basic hand tools

Miter saw

Pocket hole jig

Drill with countersink drill bit (optional)

Finish nailer

Stud finder (optional)

CUTTING LIST

- **2** 24"-long **1x10s** (top/bottom)
- **3** 27¾"-long **1x10s** (sides/center divider)
- **2** 10⅞"-long **1x2s** (back supports)
- **1** 24" x 29¼" piece of ¼" plywood (optional back)
- **2** 8½"-long **1x2s** (top sides)
- **1** 25½"-long **1x2** (top front)

Molding cut to fit

- **4** 10⅞"-long **1x10** (shelves)

DIMENSIONS

25½"

10"

30"

· **BUILT BY** ·
ASHLEY TURNER
www.shanty-2-chic.com

The simple trim and the open shelves on this project lend themselves to endless decorating possibilities. I caulked the spaces between the trim so that it would look like one piece. Then I finished the shelf with a satin latex paint and distressed the edges with a 220-grit sanding block and a dark stain.

1 BUILD THE BOX

On the top and bottom pieces, mark location of center joint. If you are using pocket holes, drill ¾" (2cm) pocket holes on both ends of sides and divider. Apply glue to end grains of sides and divider. Fasten sides and dividers to top and bottom with either 1¼" (3cm) pocket hole screws, 2" (5cm) nails, or 2" (5cm) countersunk screws.

TIP If you have a larger drill measuring more than 10" (25.5cm) long, you may wish to drill shelf pin holes before assembling the box.

2 BACK SUPPORTS

Drill a ¾" (2cm) pocket hole on each end of the back supports if using pocket holes. Apply glue to ends and top edge of back supports. Place in project, flush to the back. Attach with pocket holes if using, or attach through top and sides with glue and 2" (5cm) finish nails.

3 BACK

Apply glue to back edges of the project. Place back plywood on the project and nail down with 1¼" (3cm) nails. Find the location of center divider and nail the back to the center divider.

4 TOP SIDES

Using a scrap piece of 1x stock as a guide (1x stock is ¾" [2cm] thick), overhang the side trim ¾" (2cm) on top, and inset the front of the side trim ¾" (2cm) from the front of the box. Glue and nail down with 1¼" (3cm) nails.

5 TOP FRONT

Apply glue to the top ¾" (2cm) of the project. Place the top front on the glue and nail it down with 1¼" (3cm) nails. Also nail two 2" (5cm) nails through each end of the top into the end grain of side trim for added support.

6 DECORATIVE MOLDING

For an added touch, cut the molding, mitering ends at a 45-degree angle around the sides to create pretty corners. Use glue and 1¼" (3cm) nails to attach it.

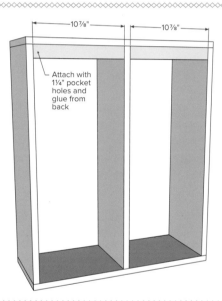

1

24"

11⅝"   11⅝"

27¾"

2

10⅞"   10⅞"

Attach with 1¼" pocket holes and glue from back

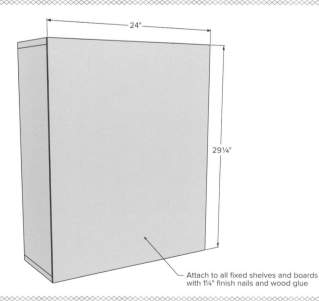

3

24"

29¼"

Attach to all fixed shelves and boards with 1¼" finish nails and wood glue

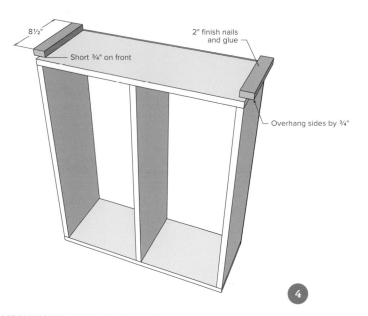

8½"

Short ¾" on front

2" finish nails and glue

Overhang sides by ¾"

4

7 **SHELF PINS**

Mark your desired location of shelves, and drill shelf pin holes. Refer to the shelf pins' packaging for hole placement, size, and depth. Insert shelf pins and place the shelves in the project.

HANGING

Hang the shelf by drilling at least two holes through the back support into a stud in the wall. Or you can hang the shelves with a heavy-duty hanging kit.

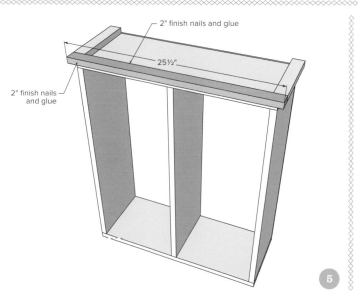

2" finish nails and glue

25½"

2" finish nails and glue

5

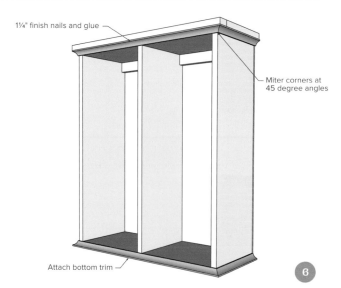

1¼" finish nails and glue

Miter corners at 45 degree angles

Attach bottom trim

6

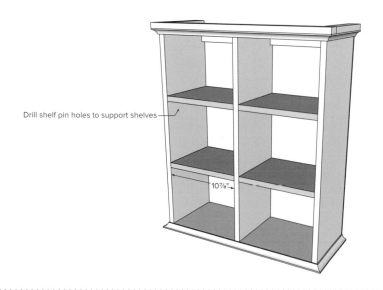

Drill shelf pin holes to support shelves

10⅞"

7

NOTE

Shelf pins can also be drilled by taping a ¼" (6mm) drill bit ¼" (6mm) from the end of the bit to drill holes ¼" (6mm) deep and ¼" (6mm) in diameter. Just make sure you drill the holes level with each other to avoid tippy or unlevel shelves.

· **BUILT BY** ·
CRYSTAL ROSE
thereadinggirl.com

❝ This kitchen island puts the *fun* in functional! The casters allow for mobility on busy days in the kitchen when floor and counter space are at a premium. The ability to build to size and finish to taste means that regardless of the shape or size of a kitchen, there is always room for a little style with this island. And for less than what is often spent on a single trip to the grocery store, this is the best use of $200 that our kitchen has ever seen! ❞

PROJECT N° 16

KITCHEN ISLAND

THIS ISLAND IS GORGEOUS AND SUBSTANTIAL,
with a wood top and tons of storage. I love its
farmhouse-meets-industrial appeal. You can park
stools at it for added eating space or roll it out
of the way—or even outdoors—for entertaining.
The farmhouse-style kitchen island requires the
purchase of four turned table legs with stretcher
block (the flat part at the base) and four caster
wheels.

Due to the high-use and extra-strength
requirements, I strongly recommend building this
kitchen island entirely with pocket hole joints as
laid out in the plan.

SHOPPING LIST

- **2** 8'-long 1x4s
- **5** 10'-long 1x6s
- **1** 6'-long 1x6
- **6** 8'-long 2x4s
- Wood glue
- 2½" pocket hole screws
- 1¼" pocket hole screws
- 2" screws to fasten top down (or use 1¼" pocket hole screws)
- 2" finishing nails
- **4** 3½" x 29¼" farmhouse table legs with stretcher block for attaching bottom shelf
- **4** 5"- diameter caster wheels
- Finishing supplies

TOOLS

Basic hand tools

Pocket hole jig

Finish nailer

Drill

Circular saw or other saw for cutting crosscuts

CUTTING LIST

- **4** 22"-long **2x4s** (end aprons)
- **4** 60"-long **2x4s** (side aprons)
- **8** 24"-long **2x4s** (supports)
- **10** 60"-long **1 x 6s** (bottom shelf top boards)
- **2** 33"-long **1x6s** (tabletop breadboard ends)
- **2** 60"-long **1x4s** (lower-shelf sides)
- **2** 22"-long **1x4s** (lower-shelf ends)

DIMENSIONS

33" 71" 36" 21¼"

1 END APRONS

Start by drilling 1½" (3.8cm) two pocket holes on each end of the end aprons. Then center the end aprons on the legs as shown and attach with 2½" (6.5cm) pocket hole screws. Note: If you wish to fasten the top down with ¾" (2cm) pocket holes, drill pocket holes along the top edge of the end aprons, on the inside only, pointing upward. Then attach the top with 1¼" (3cm) pocket hole screws and glue.

2 SIDE APRONS

Follow the instructions above for attaching the side aprons. Note: If you wish to fasten the top down with pocket holes, drill pocket holes along the top edge of the side aprons, on the inside only, set for ¾" (2cm) stock.

3 SUPPORTS

Now attach the supports with 1½" (3.8cm) pocket holes drilled on both ends and 2½" (6.5cm) pocket hole screws. **Note:** If you wish to fasten the top down with pocket holes, drill pocket holes along the top edge of the supports, on the inside only, set for ¾" (2cm) stock.

4 TABLETOP

Build the tabletop as shown in diagram with ¾" (2cm) pocket holes. By building the tabletop first, you will get a nice tight finish between the boards. Use 1¼" (3cm) pocket hole screws.

5 BOTTOM SHELF

Drill pocket holes as noted in the diagram for the bottom shelf, using ¾" (2cm) pocket holes and 1¼" (3cm) pocket hole screws.

6 TOP/SHELF PLACEMENT

Place the shelf and top on the project. Glue and nail down with 2" (5cm) finishing nails.

7 CASTER WHEELS

With the island upside down, place the caster wheels at the bottom of the legs. Screw on as directed in the caster wheel instructions.

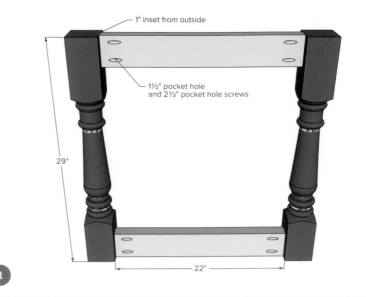

1" inset from outside

1½" pocket hole and 2½" pocket hole screws

29"

22"

1

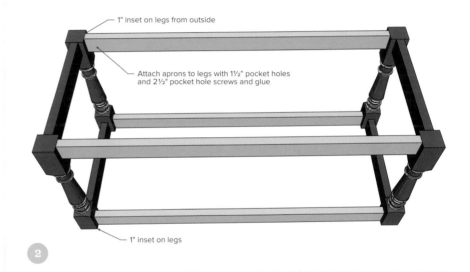

1" inset on legs from outside

Attach aprons to legs with 1½" pocket holes and 2½" pocket hole screws and glue

1" inset on legs

2

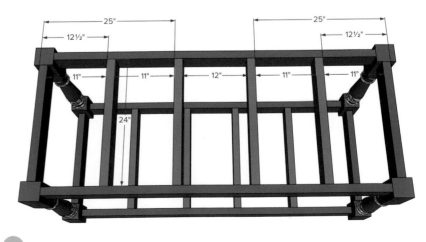

25"   25"

12½"   12½"

11"   11"   12"   11"   11"

24"

3

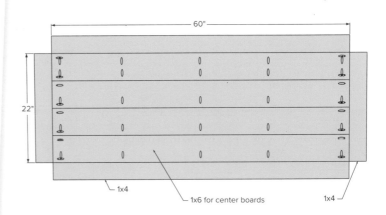

4

1x4

1x6 for center boards

1x4

5

· CRYSTAL'S TIP ·

Buy a pocket hole jig—it is worth its weight in gold, especially for this project. I had never used this handy tool before building the kitchen island, and it undoubtedly reduces the total project time/potential frustration level by at least half.

When assembling the top and bottom shelves, lay out the corresponding boards on a flat surface and place them together according to best fit—just as you would a puzzle. You may notice that some boards are curved, are crooked, or may even have a cosmetic flaw that you would prefer be on the underside. Once you find the perfect combination, number each board in order with a light pencil mark. This will ensure that your final product is sturdy, level, and pretty too.

Fit top and shelf on frame and screw down with 2" screws and wood glue to 2x4 frame. You can also hide all screw holes by using pocket holes drilled through 2x4 supports on underside

6

7
OFFICE & CRAFT ROOM

LEFT: Leaning shelves · ABOVE RIGHT:
Project table · BELOW: Storage daybed

This is one of my favorite chapters

of the book, because quite simply, the craft room or office is where I spend the majority of my time at home. The furniture projects I've chosen for this chapter include the expandable sewing table and the craft table with storage, a favorite on my website. I've updated the storage bed plans from an earlier design to decrease the cost and simplify the building. I also added a plan for a secretary that can help you create office space in any room of your home.

LEFT: Expandable sewing table
ABOVE RIGHT: Secretary

THE MOST DIFFICULT PART OF STARTING ANY

new craft project for me is, first, finding an available table to work on, and then having all my tools and supplies at hand. Our family life is put on pause until I can complete my project and clear the clutter, so when I designed this sewing table, I was motivated to create a table that could be rolled from room to room, a table that could be pushed aside and act as a console and then expanded quickly to create a temporary workspace. This table is sized to fit a sewing machine and notions; you can even hang a cutting board on the side.

SHOPPING LIST

- **2** 8'-long 1x3s
- **1** sheet of ¾" plywood, MDF, or other sheet goods
- Wood glue
- Wood filler
- **2"** screws or 1¼" pocket hole screws
- **4** 2" caster wheels with an overall clearance of 2½"
- **5** sets of ¾" x 2½" narrow-profile or surface-mount hinges

TOOLS

Basic hand tools

Circular saw

Drill

Pocket hole jig or countersink bit

CUTTING LIST

- **1** 15½" x 32" piece of ¾" plywood or MDF (center top)
- **2** 26¾" x 32" pieces of ¾" plywood or MDF (sides)
- **2** 12" x 32" pieces of ¾" plywood or MDF (shelf bottom)
- **2** 20" x 32" pieces of ¾" plywood or MDF (leaves)
- **4** 29¼"-long 1x3s (legs)

Note: You may wish to cut legs to fit depending on height of caster wheels.

DIMENSIONS

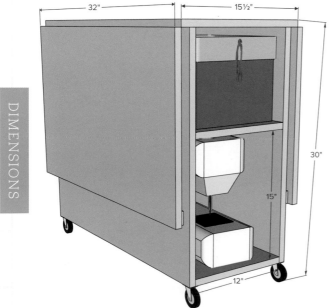

The sewing table is 30" tall x 32" deep x 14" wide (76cm x 81cm x 35.5cm) when folded down. When expanded, the sewing table top is 55½" wide x 32" deep x 30" tall (141cm x 81cm x 76cm).

This table collapses into a console with storage.

· BUILT BY ·
BROOK WILHELMSEN
www.beingbrook.com

" I'm a military spouse who has moved eleven times in the last fourteen years. My goal is to 'Create Awesome' no matter where I live. I love that this sewing table is collapsible, making it easy to set up your sewing project almost anywhere!

I primed and then painted the sewing table with two coats of coral paint, then applied two coats of polyacrylic on the tabletop to give that surface more durability. "

1 CUTTING PLYWOOD

Cut plywood with a circular saw into three pieces, each measuring 32" wide x 48" long (81cm x 122cm). From these pieces, make remaining plywood cuts per cutting layout diagrams and cutting list.

2 BUILDING THE STORAGE CENTER

Mark placement of center shelves on the sides. Predrill screw holes in preparation for attaching. Apply glue, and attach center shelves to sides. Mark the top piece 1" (2.5cm) in from sides of top, and attach to the top of the project with glue and screws. You can alternatively use ¾" (2cm) pocket holes and 1¼" (3cm) pocket hole screws and glue.

3 ATTACH WHEELS

Turn storage center upside down on its top. Position the caster wheels on the base of the storage center. Mark the screw hole locations and predrill holes to avoid splitting the wood. Attach wheels with screws as described in package instructions.

4 ATTACH LEAVES

With storage center still resting on its top (upside down), position the leaves next to the storage center, lined up with top side edges. Attach hinges to the underside of the top and leaves.

5 LEGS

The legs are attached to the underside of the leaves with hinges as shown in diagram. Because caster wheels can vary in overall height, you may wish to cut your legs to fit exactly the overall height of the table.

Flip the table over to right side up, and expand to ensure legs are the correct height. Additional hardware can be added to lock the sides in place (try a sliding bolt lock or a hook-eye closure).

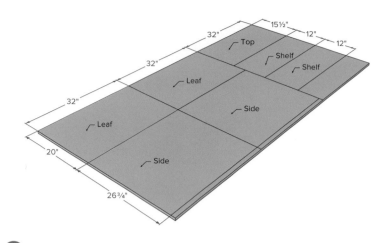

1

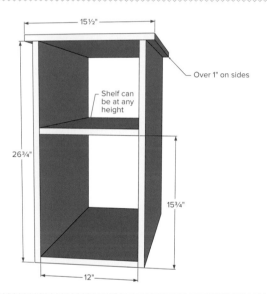

2

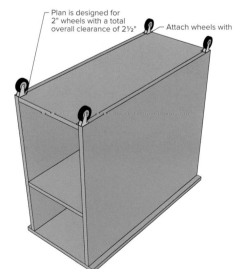

3

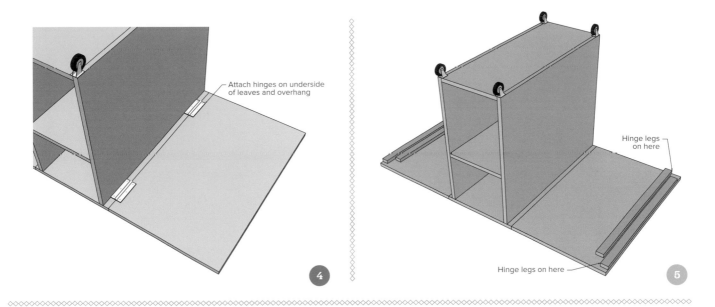

Attach hinges on underside of leaves and overhang

4

Hinge legs on here

Hinge legs on here

5

" This is a wonderful piece of furniture that functions as an organizational unit or as a display for favorite items. The design is very versatile and can be incorporated into many decor styles. "

Different depth shelves are perfect for storing all sorts of supplies.

SHOPPING LIST

- **6** 8'-long 1x4s
- **1** sheet ¾" plywood, MDF, or other sheet goods
- Wood glue
- 1¼" pocket hole screws
- 1¼" finish nails
- 2" finish nails
- Heavy-duty picture-hanging kit for securing to wall

TOOLS

- Basic hand tools
- Circular saw
- Drill
- Pocket hole jig
- Countersink bit
- Finish nailer
- Jigsaw

CUTTING LIST

- **2** 77⅜"-long **1x4s** (legs)
- **1** 17¼" x 31½" piece of ¾" plywood or MDF (shelf bottom)
- **1** 14¼" x 31½" piece of ¾" plywood or MDF (shelf bottom)
- **1** 12¼" x 31½" piece of ¾" plywood or MDF (shelf bottom)
- **1** 10¼" x 31½" piece of ¾" plywood or MDF (shelf bottom)
- **1** 8¼" x 31½" piece of ¾" plywood or MDF (shelf bottom)
- **2** 17¼"-long **1x4s** (shelf sides)
- **2** 14¼"-long **1x4s** (shelf sides)
- **2** 12¼"-long **1x4s** (shelf sides)
- **2** 10¼"-long **1x4s** (shelf sides)
- **2** 8¼"-long **1x4s** (shelf sides)
- **5** 33"-long **1x4** (shelf backs)
- **5** 33"-long **1x4s** (shelf supports)

CUTTING PLYWOOD

Cut plywood into two pieces 31½" x 48" (80cm x 122cm). Then from these pieces cut the individual pieces.

TIP Ask your hardware store to make the initial cuts to save time.

PROJECT Nº18
LEANING BOOKSHELVES

I CAN'T THINK OF A ROOM IN MY HOME that couldn't fit, use, and benefit from these leaning wall shelves. Save space and add style in your study, bathroom, kitchen, or entryway with these easy-to-build, inexpensive shelves.

DIMENSIONS

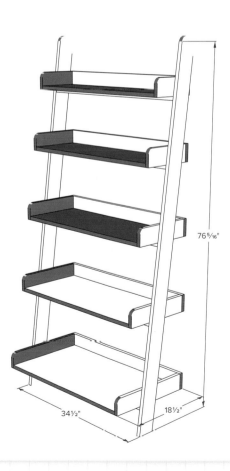

76 ⁵⁄₁₆"

34½"

18½"

1 LEGS

Mark legs for shelf support placement carefully as shown in large diagram. Consider that each mark is at an angle.

TIP Use the scrap block cut from the leg bottom to help you mark the legs. Make sure to keep placement parallel as noted on diagram.

2 SHELF SIDES

Attach shelf sides to shelf bottom with either 2" (5cm) screws or glue and 2" finish nails, or using ¾" (2cm) pocket holes and 1¼" (3cm) pocket hole screws from the underside. Match each shelf to the matching trim pieces.

3 SHELF BACKS

Once sides are attached to all shelves, attach back trim either with ¾" (2cm) pocket holes and 1¼" (3cm) pocket hole screws and glue, or with 2" (5cm) finish nails and glue or 2" (5cm) countersunk screws and glue. Also attach back to shelf sides.

4 ROUND CORNERS

Round the top front corners of the shelves with a jigsaw to soften. Sand all edges cut with a jigsaw.

TIP Use the scrap from the first rounded corner as a pattern for all remaining shelf fronts.

5 FRAME

Use the lines drawn in on the legs to position the supports in the correct location. Attach the shelf supports to the frame sides using either ¾" (2cm) pocket holes and 1¼" (3cm) pocket hole screws or glue and 2" (5cm) nails and screws.

ASSEMBLY

Attach heavy-duty picture-hanging kit hardware to the back of the top shelf support, and secure it to the wall. Then slide the shelves in place, starting with the largest (bottom) shelf and working upward. Mark placement and remove. Apply glue and replace. Screw the shelves to the supports and sides with 1¼" (3cm) screws.

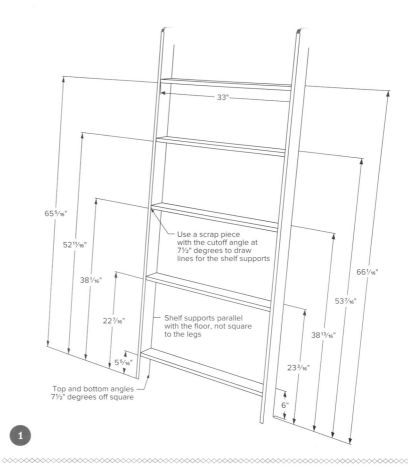

Use a scrap piece with the cutoff angle at 7½ degrees to draw lines for the shelf supports

Shelf supports parallel with the floor, not square to the legs

Top and bottom angles 7½" degrees off square

33"

65⁵/₁₆"

52¹¹/₁₆"

38¹/₁₆"

22⁷/₁₆"

5⁵/₁₆"

66¹/₁₆"

53⁷/₁₆"

38¹³/₁₆"

23³/₁₆"

6"

1

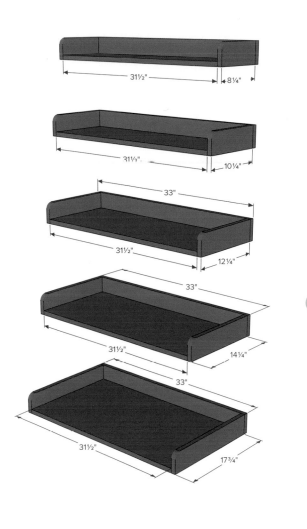

31½"   8¼"

31½"   10¼"

33"
31½"   12¼"

33"
31½"   14¼"

33"
31½"   17¾"

2

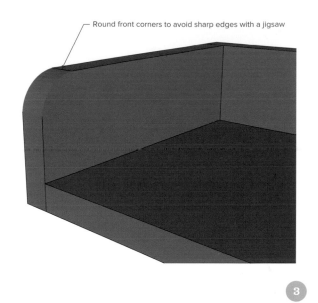

Round front corners to avoid sharp edges with a jigsaw

3

4

· FINISHING ·

"We applied two coats of Benjamin Moore Marscarpone in semi-gloss allowing each coat to dry thoroughly."

modern
PROJECT TABLE

SHOPPING LIST

1 sheet of ¾" plywood or MDF

3 8'-long 1x12s

1 12'-long 1x12 (cut ends and dividers from this board)

1 12'-long 1x10

7 8'-long 1x2s

2 8'-long 2x2s

Wood glue

Wood filler

1¼" finish nails

2" finish nails

2" wood screws

TOOLS

Basic hand tools

Circular saw or other saw for making crosscuts

Finish nailer

Drill

CUTTING LIST

2 37¼"-long **1x12s** (bookshelf tops)

2 36½"-long **1x12s** (bookshelf bottom)

2 33½"-long **1x12s** (bookshelf ends)

2 32"-long **1x12s** (bookshelf divider)

4 27¼"-long **1x12s** (large shelves)

4 34¼"-long **1x10s** (small bookshelf sides)

4 8½"-long **1x12s** (cubby shelves)

8 27¾"-long **1x2s** (large shelf trim)

4 13"-long **1x2s** (small shelf top and bottom trim)

8 31¼"-long **1x2s** (side trim)

4 8½"-long **2x2s** (floating base ends)

4 36½"-long **2x2s** (floating base sides)

1 38" x 54" piece of ¾" plywood or MDF (tabletop)

4 10"-long **2x2s** (tabletop floating base ends)

4 36½"-long **1x2s** (tabletop floating base sides)

THERE ARE SO MANY MORE URGENT ROOMS
to furnish, such as the living room and bedroom, that often your most creative space—your craft room—is neglected. Who can afford to spend thousands of dollars on that perfect craft table? Fortunately you can build your own! This craft-table plan features six large shelves and six smaller shelves. At bar height, there is more room to store supplies, and it requires less bend when cutting. The increased height also increases under-table storage, and adds valuable storage space at the perfect height for crafting.

DIMENSIONS

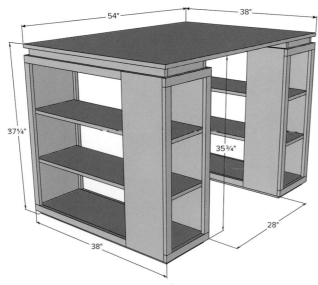

The project table measures 54" wide by 38" deep by 37¼" tall (137cm x 96.5cm x 95cm). Seating is bar height.

"I am a stay-at-home mom who loves photography, cooking, and painting everything in sight! My husband is a tech sergeant and an air-traffic controller in the United States Air Force, and together we like to tackle all kinds of DIY projects. This project table was the most elaborate one yet, but every time I look at it, I think, 'Wow, we built that!' It really gives you a great sense of accomplishment!"

Keep supplies within easy reach, but free of your workspace!

1 FRAMING THE BOOKSHELVES

Start by building a box for the bookshelves as shown in the diagram. You can use your preferred fastening method, anything from finish nails to countersunk screws to ¾" (2cm) pocket holes and 1¼" (3cm) pocket hole screws and glue. If you use finish nails, choose glue and 2" (5cm) nails. Measure carefully and mark each joint, building from the inside outward. You will need to build two bookshelves.

2 SIDES

Lay the 1x10s over the exposed sides, with the top flush to the top of the bookshelf. If your 1x10 boards are narrower than expected, simply trim the top and bottom shelves down to fit. Apply glue and fasten with 2" (5cm) finish nails.

3 CUBBY SHELVES

Mark the location of your cubby shelves and apply glue to the joints. Slide the shelves in place and attach through the sides with 2" (5cm) finish nails.

4 SHELF TRIM

Apply glue to the top and bottom edges and attach shelf trim with 1¼" (3cm) finish nails.

5 SIDE TRIM

Finish the bookshelves by applying glue to the outside edges and attaching side trim with 1¼" (3cm) finish nails.

6 SMALL SHELF FRONT/ BOTTOM TRIM

Apply glue and attach trim with 1¼" (3cm) finish nails.

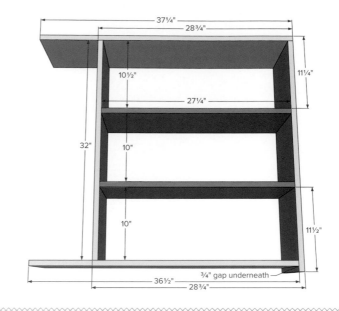

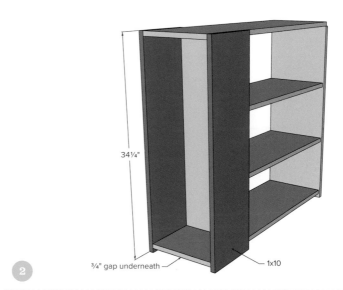

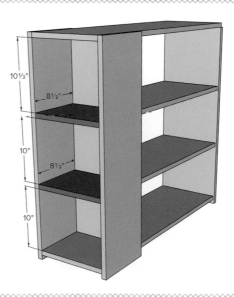

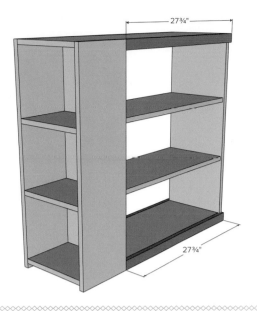

27¾"

27¾"

4

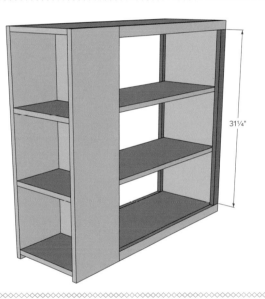

31¼"

5

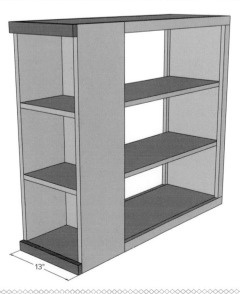

13"

6

7 SMALL SHELF SIDE TRIM

Apply glue and attach final trim pieces with 1¼" (3cm) finish nails.

8 BOOKSHELF BASE

On the bottom of each bookshelf, apply glue to the 2x2 floating base sides, and nail down with 2" (5cm) finish nails to the bottom of the bookshelves.

9 BOOKSHELF BASE ENDS

Fit the remaining base ends to the base sides, and apply glue. Nail down with 2" (5cm) finish nails. Also nail base ends to base sides. This will complete the floating bases for the bookshelves. Set the bookshelves aside; it's time to work on the tabletop.

10 TABLETOP BASE ENDS

On the underside of the tabletop, measure and mark the location of the tabletop floating base ends. Attach the tabletop base ends with wood glue and 2" (5cm) finish nails.

11 TABLETOP BASE SIDE

Attach the remaining long floating base sides to the base ends as shown in the diagram. Use wood glue and 2" (5cm) finish nails.

12 ASSEMBLY

To assemble the project table, set the tabletop on the bookcases, adjusting to fit. Drill pilot holes, and screw through the underside of the bookshelves with 2" (5cm) screws into the tabletop base to secure it.

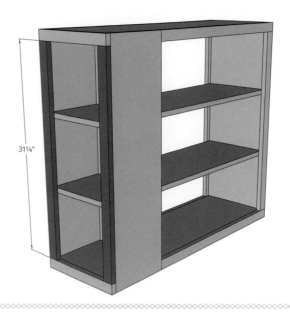

7

31¼"

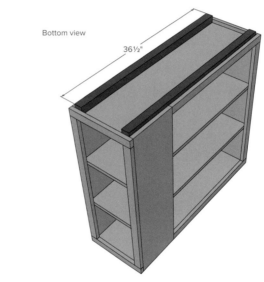

8

Bottom view

36½"

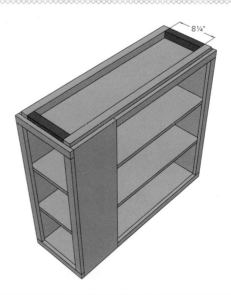

9

8¼"

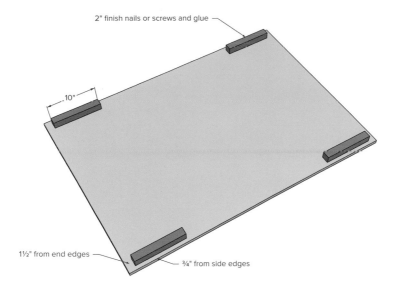

2" finish nails or screws and glue

10"

1½" from end edges

¾" from side edges

10

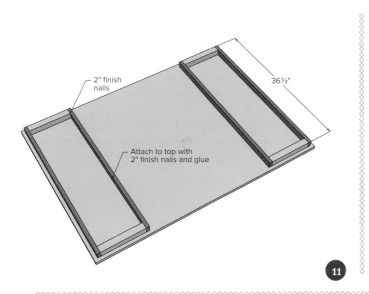

2" finish nails

36½"

Attach to top with 2" finish nails and glue

11

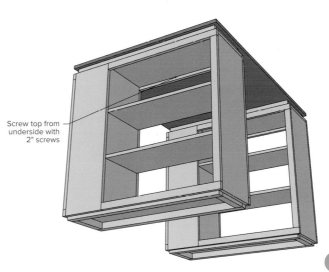

Screw top from underside with 2" screws

12

This project table also looks great in blue, the color Brook Wilhelmsen chose to paint her version.

This fits a standard twin mattress.

· BUILT BY ·
LAYLA PALMER
www.theletteredcottage.com

"We live in the deep South (Prattville, Alabama, to be exact), and we share a passion for writing and our love of older homes. It also seems sort of appropriate that the first letters of each word of our blog are T, L, and C, because our fixer-upper could definitely use lots of tender lovin' care."

YOU ARE
pure
POTENTIAL

SELECTO
EAST TENNESSEE
PACKING CO.
PURE LARD

PROJECT
N°20

storage
DAYBED

YOU WON'T BELIEVE JUST HOW MUCH
space a storage bed can create in a room!
These storage bases can hold about the
same amount as a very large bookshelf,
and they are perfect for storing everything
from books to extra blankets to baskets
full of less-than-attractive objects. I have
redesigned this popular plan to be easier
to build, to minimize materials, and to make
the bed more versatile. Every side of the
storage daybed is finished, so you can place
it in the middle of the room for a reading
spot or squeeze it into a nook in a reading
room, as Layla has done.

SHOPPING LIST

- **5** 8'-long **1x12s**
- **5** 8'-long **1x2s**
- **6** 8'-long **1x3s**
- **2** 8'-long **2x2s**
- **1** sheet of ¼" plywood or hardboard
- Wood glue
- ¾" finish nails
- 1¼" finish nails
- 2" finish nails
- 1¼" screws
- 2" screws
- 1¼" pocket hole screws (optional)

TOOLS

- Basic hand tools
- Circular saw or other saw for making crosscuts
- Finish nailer
- Pocket hole jig (recommended)
- Drill
- Countersink bit

CUTTING LIST

- **4** 12¾"-long **1x12s** (storage dividers)
- **4** 15¼"-long **1x12s** (storage ends)
- **2** 74½"-long **1x12s** (storage tops)
- **2** 73"-long **1x12s** (storage bottoms)
- **2** 75"-long **1x2s** (storage top trim)
- **2** 75"-long **1x3s** (storage base trim)
- **14** 12"-long **1x2s** (vertical trim for storage and end panels/dividers)
- **2** 74½" x 16" piece of ¼" plywood (storage backs)
- **2** 74½"-long **2x2s** (cleats)
- **2** 40½"-long **1x2s** (end panel tops)
- **2** 40½"-long **1x3s** (end panel bottoms)
- **2** 39" x 16" pieces of ¼" plywood (end panel backs)
- **14** 16"-long **1x3s** (slats)

*Recommend to add slats to fit.

DIMENSIONS

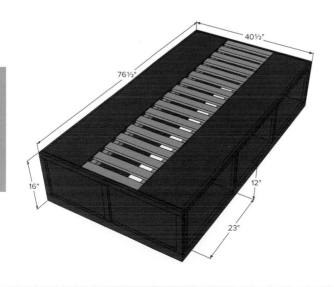

40½"

76½"

16"

12"

23"

1 PLYWOOD CUTTING

Cut ¼" (6mm) plywood into strips 16" wide by 96" long (40.5cm x 244cm).

TIP Ask the hardware store to make long cuts for you if you do not have a table saw. Once plywood is cut into strips, simply cut strips crosswise to the length of pieces needed to build the bed.

2 STORAGE BOXES

This bed is just two big bookcases on their side. We will start by building the bookcase boxes, as depicted in the diagrams. Attach dividers to the top and bottom of the storage bases by measuring and marking the location as shown in the diagram. Notice that the top is longer than the bottom, and measurements do differ. Predrill holes and attach. Build two.

3 FACE FRAME

Attach trim to the face of the box using wood glue and 1¼" (3cm) finish nails. The ends of the face frame extend over the storage box ¼" (6mm) on each end.

If using a pocket hole jig, build the face frame first with ¾" (2cm) pocket holes, and attach with glue and 1¼" (3cm) pocket hole screws. Then attach the prebuilt face frame to the storage box with 1¼" (3cm) finish nails.

4 BACK

Adjust each storage base for square, and apply glue to all back edges. Attach back to storage base using glue and 1¼" (3cm) finish nails.

5 BACK CLEATS

Mark the back of each storage box ¾" (2cm) down from the top.

TIP Use a 1x scrap as a guide, noting 1x material is ¾" (2cm) thick.

Predrill holes in the cleats, positioning the predrilled holes to screw into the dividers and ends in the storage bases. Attach the cleat to the back of the storage bases ¾" (2cm) down from top using 2½" (6.5cm) screws.

6 END FRAMES

Build end frames with ¾" (2cm) pocket holes and 1¼" (3cm) pocket hole screws or by carefully predrilling holes for 2" (5cm) screws.

TIP Use a clamp to ensure boards remain lined up. Adjust for square.

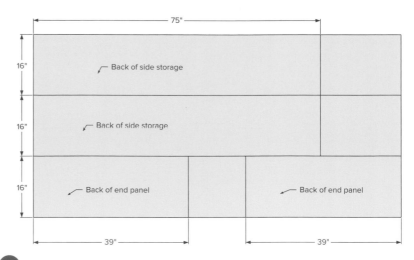

1

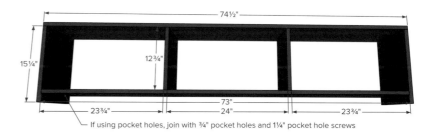

If using pocket holes, join with ¾" pocket holes and 1¼" pocket hole screws

2

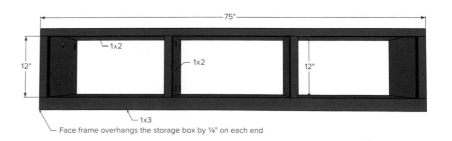

Face frame overhangs the storage box by ¼" on each end

3

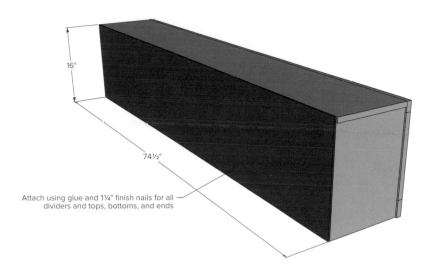

16"

74½"

Attach using glue and 1¼" finish nails for all
dividers and tops, bottoms, and ends

4

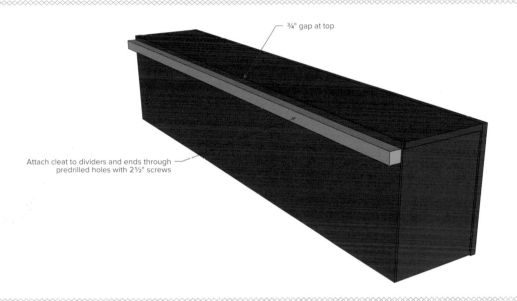

¾" gap at top

Attach cleat to dividers and ends through
predrilled holes with 2½" screws

5

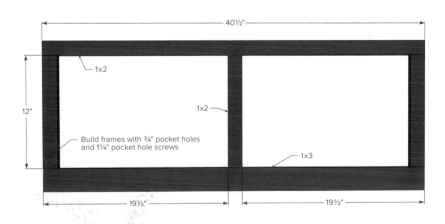

40½"

1x2

12"

1x2

Build frames with ¾" pocket holes
and 1¼" pocket hole screws

1x3

19½"

19½"

6

7 END BACKS

Mark each end ¾" (2cm) from the outside edge. Ensure there is at least a ¾" (2cm) gap on each end frame not covered by plywood. Attach the plywood back with glue and ¾" (2cm) finish nails.

8 ASSEMBLY

This bed is designed to assemble in the designated room for easy transportation. You may wish to assemble to finish it, disassemble, and then reassemble in your room. The ends are screwed to the storage bases through the inside of the storage bases. Screw through the top and bottom with 1¼" (3cm) screws. Do not use glue; this allows for future disassembly.

9 SLATS

Lay the slats approximately 2" (5cm) apart, screwing them down with 1¼" screws. Do not use glue; this enables disassembly.

TIP To convert this to a full-size bed, increase the width of the ends by 15" (38cm) and cut slats 15" (38cm) longer.

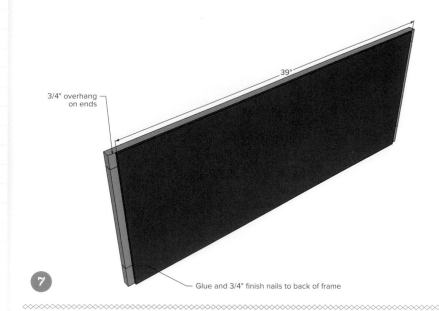

7

3/4" overhang on ends

39"

Glue and 3/4" finish nails to back of frame

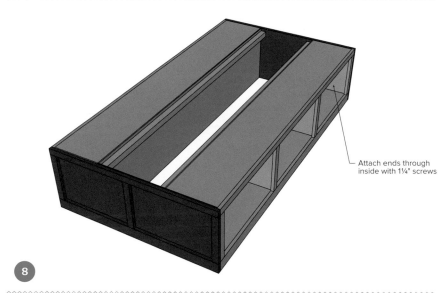

8

Attach ends through inside with 1¼" screws

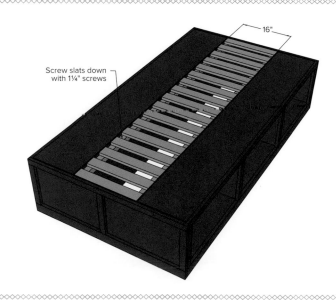

9

16"

Screw slats down with 1¼" screws

SECRETARY

CREATE A BEAUTIFUL OFFICE SPACE

anywhere in your home with this secretary. Featuring a flip-down face and two shelves concealed by cabinets, it assures that all of your home-office needs can be concealed in a small space.

SHOPPING LIST

- **1** sheet of ¼" plywood
- **3** 8'-long 1x12s
- **5** 8'-long 2x2s
- **1** 8'-long 1x2
- **1** 6'-long 1x4
- **1** sheet of ¾" plywood cut into strips 11½" wide by 8' long or 3 8'-long 1x12s (Note: Most 1x12 boards are 11¼" wide, and you will need to make minor adjustments as noted in plan to account for this difference.)

Wood glue

¾" finish nails

1¼" finish nails

2" finish nails

1¼" pocket hole screws

2" screws

3 sets Euro-style surface-mount full-overlay/inset hinges

Cabinet clasp or catch

Hinge supports or chain (optional)

Finishing supplies

TOOLS

Drill

Finish nailer

Circular saw or other saw for making crosscuts

Pocket hole jig

Jigsaw

Drill

CUTTING LIST

- **4** 11½"-long **1x2s** (side trim, cut to width of 1x12) **(Note: 1x12 boards can vary in width. This plan expects your 1x12 boards to be 11½" wide.)**
- **2** 37¼"-long **1x12s** (sides)
- **3** 32"-long **1x12s** (shelves)
- **4** 43¼"-long **2x2s** (legs)
- **6** 32"-long **2x2s** (shelf trim)
- **1** 11¼"-long **2x2** (cut to width of 1x12)
- **1** 37"-long **1x12** (top)
- **1** 37"-long **1x2** (top back)
- **1** 37"-long **1x3** (top front)
- **1** 32"-long **1x4** (base trim front)
- **2** 11¼"-long **1x4s** (base trim sides, cut to width of 1x12)
- **1** 31¾"-long **1x12** (secretary front)

1x3s and ¼" plywood for doors and back

TIP Mark and drill all pocket holes prior to assembly.

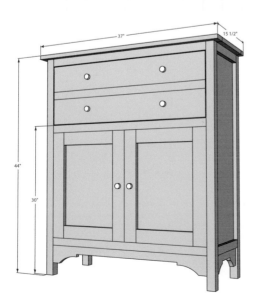

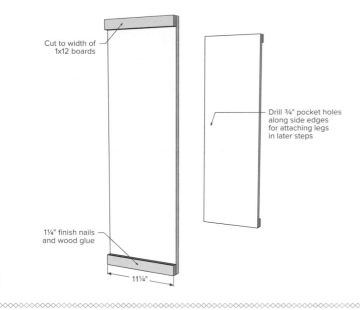

Cut to width of
1x12 boards

Drill ¾" pocket holes
along side edges
for attaching legs
in later steps

1¼" finish nails
and wood glue

11¼"

1

1 SIDE TRIM

Attach side trim with glue and 1¼" (3cm) finish nails using your finish nailer to sides at tops and bottoms, keeping edges flush.

TIP Depending on the width of your 1x12 boards, you may need to cut your trim boards down to size.

2 SHELVES

Drill ¾" (2cm) pocket holes at ends of each shelf. Mark shelf locations on the secretary sides and attach them with glue and 1¼" (3cm) pocket hole screws.

TIP This plan assumes you are using 1x12 boards that are 11¼" wide, ripped from plywood or sheet goods. If your 1x12s are not, alter the top shelf location so the distance between the shelf top and the top of the sides is equal to the width of your 1x12 board plus 1¾" (4.5cm) to create a perfect fold-down door face.

3 LEGS

Attach the legs to the sides with glue and 2" (5cm) screws, keeping top edges flush. You can alternatively attach with ¾" (2cm) pocket holes predrilled in the sides, glue and 1¼" (3cm) pocket hole screws.

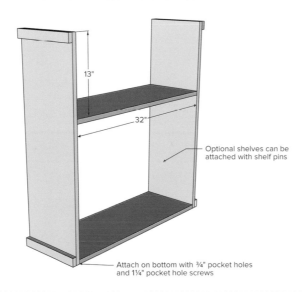

13"

32"

Optional shelves can be attached with shelf pins

Attach on bottom with ¾" pocket holes and 1¼" pocket hole screws

2

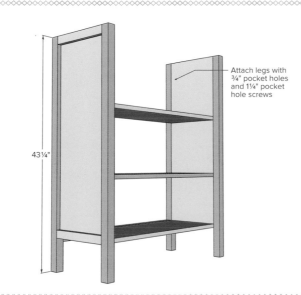

43¼"

Attach legs with ¾" pocket holes and 1¼" pocket hole screws

3

4 SHELF TRIM

Attach trim to the top, top shelf and the bottom with 2x2 shelf-trim boards. Attach them with glue and 2" (5cm) nails or screws. Also attach the legs to the ends of the shelf trim. Keep trim tops flush to shelves.

5 TOP SUPPORT

Mark the center of the top. Position the top support in place and screw to the trim sides with either 2" (5cm) screws or by adding ¾" (2cm) pocket holes and 1¼" (3cm) pocket hole screws and glue.

TIP If your 1x12 boards are not 11½" (29cm) wide, you will need to trim the top support to fit. Example: If your 1x12 boards measure 11¼" wide, your trim is then 11¼" long.

6 TOP

If using pocket holes, build the top prior to attaching it with glue, ¾" (2cm) pocket holes, and 1¼" (3cm) pocket hole screws. Screw through the top support and top-shelf trim pieces to attach the top from underneath. Use 2" (5cm) screws; keep the back flush, with the front and sides overhanging 1" (2.5cm).

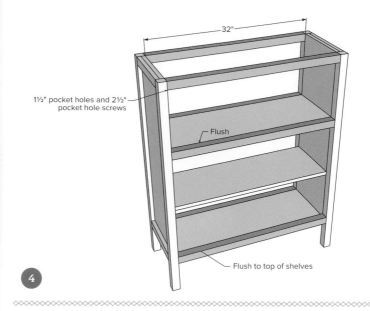

1½" pocket holes and 2½" pocket hole screws

32"

Flush

Flush to top of shelves

4

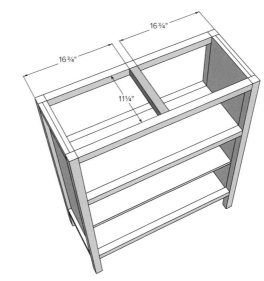

16¾"

16¾"

11¼"

5

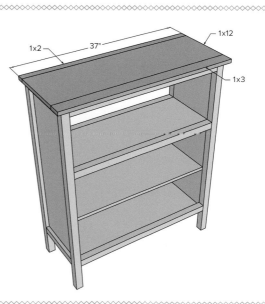

1x2

37"

1x12

1x3

6

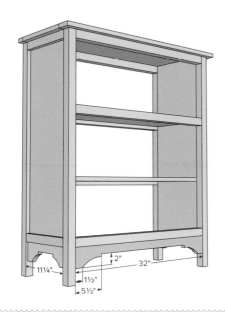

7

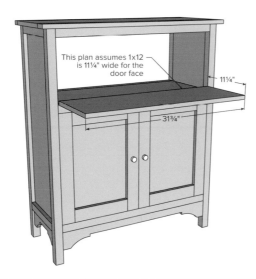

This plan assumes 1x12 is 11¼" wide for the door face

11¼"

31¾"

8

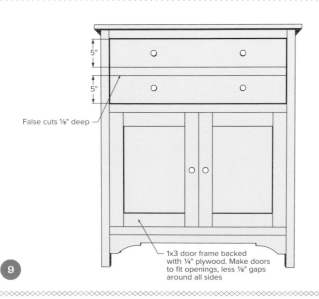

5"

5"

False cuts ⅛" deep

1x3 door frame backed with ¼" plywood. Make doors to fit openings, less ⅛" gaps around all sides

9

7 BASE TRIM

Mark base trim boards with a decorative pattern as suggested in diagram. Cut out with a jigsaw, using the first cutout as a pattern for remaining cutouts. Sand the edges cut with the jigsaw until smooth and even. Attach base trim from the back to bottom shelf and leg with ¾" (2cm) pocket holes and 1¼" (3cm) pocket hole screws and glue.

8 FLIP-DOWN DOOR

Make false cuts ⅛" (3mm) deep in the flip-down door face to make the flip-down door appear as two drawers. Attach the flip-down door to the face of the secretary using Euro-style surface-mount full-overlay/inset hinges. Keep gaps around all sides of the flip-down door even and equal at approximately ⅛" (3mm). Secure the flip-down door with either hinge supports or a chain to keep it secure when opened. Add a clasp to keep the door in place when closed.

9 DOORS

When building doors, especially inset doors, always build to fit the opening for the best overall fit. Measure the opening and divide by two. Subtract ¼" (6mm) from the width and height measurements. This measurement is your overall door size. Cut 1x3 boards to make a frame with outside dimensions equal to your overall door size. Make ¾" (2cm) pocket holes and join the boards with glue and 1¼" (3cm) pocket hole screws. Attach plywood to the back with glue and ¾" (2cm) finish nails. Attach doors with surface-mount or narrow-profile hinges, and add clasps to keep doors closed.

TIP Consider attaching hinges to the frame before attaching the door-back plywood if your hinges are designed for doors ¾" (2cm) thick.

WALL CRAFT ORGANIZER

SHOPPING LIST

- **4** 32"-long ¾" wood dowels
- **2** 8'-long 1x8s
- **1** 6'-long 1x4
- 2" screws or finish nails
- ¾" brad nails
- Hardware to hang to wall
- **1** 9"-long 1x2
- Wood glue and finishing supplies

TOOLS

Basic hand tools

Drill

¾" (2cm) spade bit

Saw for making crosscuts

Finish nailer

CUTTING LIST

- **1** 12⅜"-long **1x8** (tall vertical divider)
- **1** 6¼"-long **1x8** (short vertical divider)
- **1** 20¾"-long **1x8** (middle shelf)
- **2** 30½"-long **1x8s** (top and bottom shelves)
- **2** 30½"-long **1x4s** (top shelf back and bottom base)
- **2** 34"-long **1x8s** (sides)
- **1** 9"-long **1x2** (shelf trim, optional)
- **1** 32" x 34" ¼" plywood (back)

CREATING SYSTEMS FOR TASKS WE regularly perform is vital to organizing our homes. Who doesn't enjoy wrapping gifts? But without a dedicated spot to store wrapping paper, what should be a fun activity might become a dreaded task.

With four dowels for hanging ribbons and wrapping paper—and an ample compartment for keeping scissors, tape, bows, and even cards close at hand—this organizer keeps everything you need. This project can also be used for storing arts-and-craft supplies for children.

DIMENSIONS

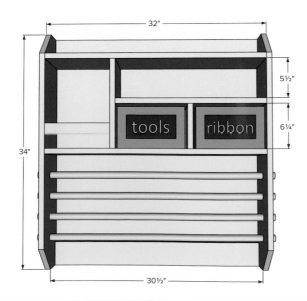

" I love that this inspires me to tackle more of my craft projects. It almost functions as a visual pin board. With small children, this is a way to have my supplies up out of reach, and I don't have to waste time dragging everything out onto the table.

   The finished project is heavy. So if you are not screwing it directly into the studs of your wall, I'd encourage you to get a hanging kit that can accommodate at least up to 100 lbs. (Finished project plus the weight of supplies you will store on it.) "

1 CENTER DIVIDERS

Begin by marking all divider joint locations on divider boards. Apply glue on ends of all boards before attaching. Because this is a wall hanging project, you can attach with glue and 2" (5cm) nails or 2" (5cm)screws. Set aside center dividers.

2 TOP SHELF

Attach top shelf to top shelf back with 2" (5cm) screws or nails and glue. Back edges are flush. You can also use ¾" (2cm) pocket hole and 1¼" (3cm) pocket hole screws and glue.

3 ATTACHING TOP SHELF

Mark location of tall vertical divider to top shelf joint on top shelf. Apply glue to top edge of tall vertical divider and attach to top shelf, keeping outside edges flush. Use either 2" (5cm) screws or nails.

4 SIDES

From sides, mark corners and cut off with a circular saw to soften edges. Mark location of holes for dowels and drill out with a ¾" (2cm) spade bit. Apply glue to exposed edges of main project and attach sides with 2" (5cm) screws or finish nails.

5 BOTTOM BASE SUPPORT AND SHELF TRIM

Apply glue to ends of bottom base and attach to sides with 2" (5cm) screws or finish nails at base of craft organizer. If adding shelf trim, apply glue to ends and attach inside tall storage compartment.

6 BACK

Attach the back plywood to the project using ¾" (2cm) nails and glue.

7 HANGING

This craft organizer is made of solid wood and will be heavy. You must hang it properly. The easiest method is to screw through the base and top-shelf back directly into a stud in your wall with screws sufficient in length. The other option in to use a heavy-duty picture-hanging kit.

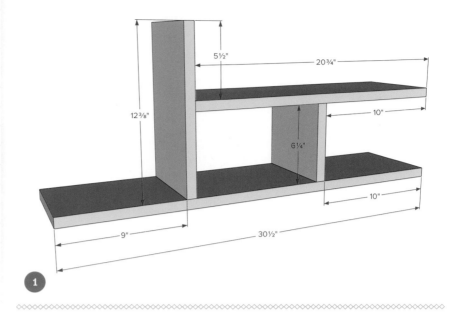

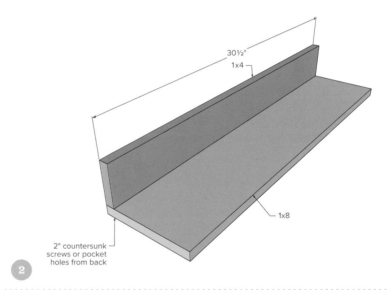

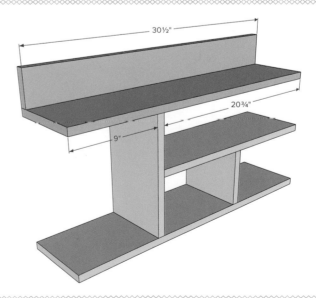

132

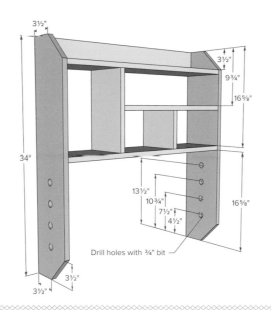

3½"
3½"
9¾"
16⅝"
34"
13½"
10¾"
7½"
4½"
16⅝"
Drill holes with ¾" bit
3½"
3½"

4

9"

30½"

5

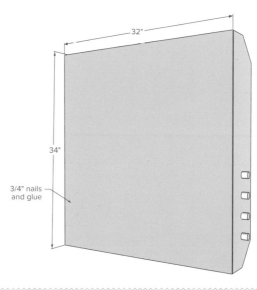

32"

34"

3/4" nails
and glue

6

Screw to stud in wall

tools   ribbon

7

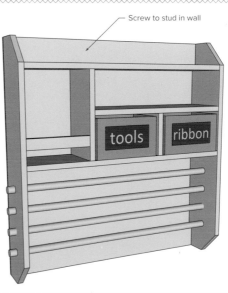

8
BEDROOM

LEFT: Farmhouse bed
BELOW: Farmhouse bedside table

When the day is over and we are

seeking rest, it's our bedroom that we turn to for refuge. You can create an organized and comfortable retreat with the plans in this chapter. Of course, the farmhouse bed plan is included, updated for simplicity and cost efficiency. I've also included plans for a simple bedside table, a versatile and grown-up upholstered headboard, and storage in a farmhouse armoire.

ABOVE RIGHT: Armoire • LEFT: Upholstered headboard

PROJECT
N° 23
farmhouse
BED

MY FARMHOUSE BED WAS THE FIRST REAL
furniture project I tackled, and as the paint dried, I just stared at it in disbelief that I made it. We still sleep in this very bed every night.

When I started blogging, this was the first plan I shared. I have since lost track of how many farmhouse beds have been built using that plan. For this book, I have improved the plan so that it is easier to build and uses fewer materials. This bed is designed to work with a standard box-spring and bed-rail system.

SHOPPING LIST

5 8'-long 1x10s

2 10'-long 1x4s

2 6'-long 4x4s

2 8'-long 2x4s

2 8'-long 2x6s

Wood glue

1¼" pocket hole screws

1¼" finish nails

2" screws

3" screws

Queen-size metal bed-rail kit

TOOLS

Basic hand tools

Pocket hole jig

Circular saw or other saw for making crosscuts

Finish nailer

CUTTING LIST

6 32"-long **1x10s** (headboard-panel boards)

6 15"-**1x10s** (footboard-panel boards)

4 55½"-long **1x4s** (panel trim)

2 54"-long **4x4s** (headboard legs)

2 21"-long **4x4s** (footboard legs)

2 62½"-long **2x4s** (top of panel/legs)

2 64½"-long **2x6s** (header)

2 **1x10s** cut to length of side rails (optional side rails)

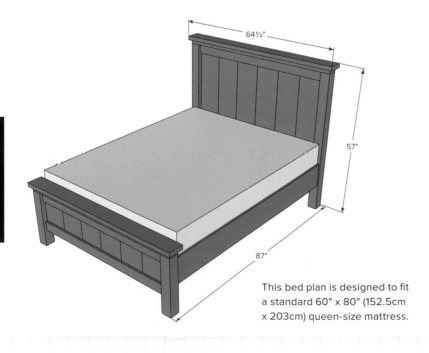

This bed plan is designed to fit a standard 60" x 80" (152.5cm x 203cm) queen-size mattress.

DIMENSIONS

· NOTE ·

The measurements given are for a queen. Modify this to a twin, full, or king by altering the width of the headboards and footboards, and the length of the side rails. Most twin beds are 21" less in width and 5" shorter than a queen. Most full beds are 6" in width and 5" shorter than a queen. Kings can vary from 16" to 20" more in width and 0" to 14" more in length than a queen.

1 PANELS

Build panels for headboard and footboard with glue, ¾" (2cm) pocket holes, and 1¼" (3cm) pocket hole screws. Drill pocket holes along top and side outside edges. Measure each panel to ensure it is 55½" (141cm) wide; trim to this measurement if it's wider.

2 PANEL TRIM

On the panel faces free of pocket holes, attach 1x4 trim boards with glue and 1¼" (3cm) finish nails.

3 LEGS

With top flush, inset panel 1" (2.5cm) from legs and attach through pocket holes previously drilled, using wood glue and 1¼" (3cm) pocket hole screws.

4 2x4 TOP

Apply glue to top edge of headboard and footboard panels and legs and attach the 2x4 top. Screw the 2x4 top to 4x4 legs using 2" (5cm) screws.

5 2x6 TOP

Mark the 2x6 top 1" (2.5cm) in from all outside edges. Apply glue to the top of the 2x4. Lay the 2x6 top on top and attach with 3" (7.5cm) screws.

6 FOOTBOARD

Construct the footboard identically to the headboard, except legs and panel boards are shorter.

BED RAILS

Determine desired height of bed and attach metal bed rails directly to legs, following instructions included with bed-frame system.

7 SIDE RAILS

Measure and cut the remaining 1x10 boards to the length of the bed rails, or the distance between the headboard and footboard. Attach the boards to the bed rails and, using ¾" (2cm) pocket holes and 1¼" (3cm) pocket hole screws, to the legs of the headboard and footboard, concealing the bed frame.

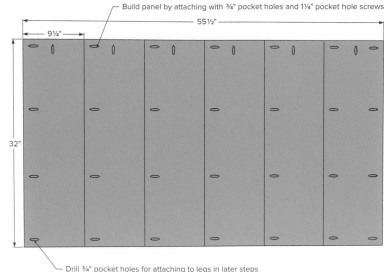

Build panel by attaching with ¾" pocket holes and 1¼" pocket hole screws

9¼"   55½"

32"

1 Drill ¾" pocket holes for attaching to legs in later steps

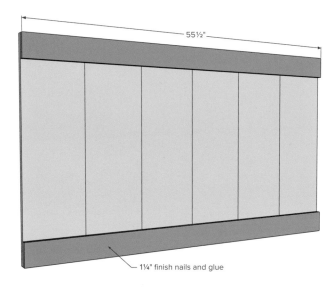

55½"

2 1¼" finish nails and glue

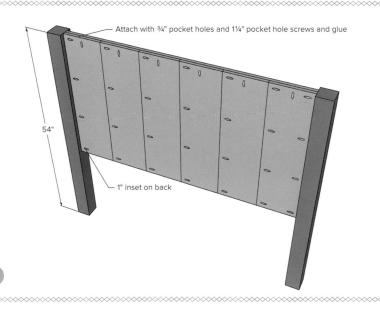

Attach with ¾" pocket holes and 1¼" pocket hole screws and glue

54"

3 1" inset on back

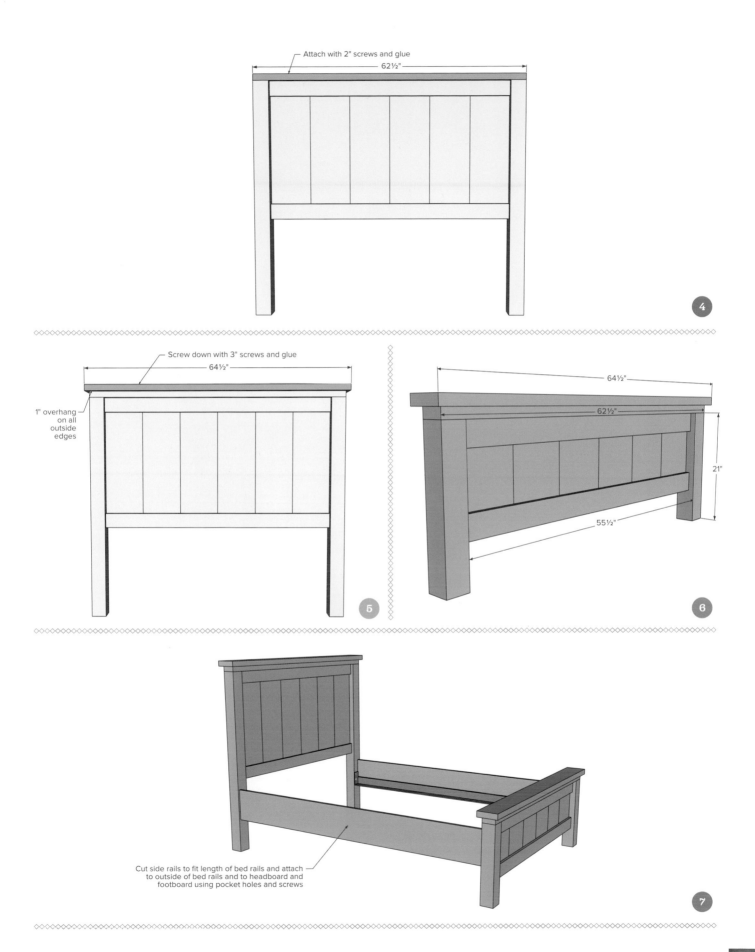

Attach with 2" screws and glue

62½"

4

Screw down with 3" screws and glue

64½"

1" overhang on all outside edges

5

64½"

62½"

21"

55½"

6

Cut side rails to fit length of bed rails and attach to outside of bed rails and to headboard and footboard using pocket holes and screws

7

BUILT BY
AMANDA CLARK

farmhouse
BEDSIDE TABLE

THIS SIMPLE TABLE IS THE PERFECT

height for beside your bed or for an end table next to a sofa. It features a roomy drawer on metal slides and a large bottom shelf perfect for a basket, books, or even a spare quilt. The farmhouse bedside table matches the entryway console to create easy living-room occasional tables that match.

SHOPPING LIST

- **1** 8'-long 2x2
- **2** 8'-long 1x2s
- **1** 8'-long 1x4
- **1** 2'-long 1x6
- **¼** sheet of ¼" plywood
- **1** 72"-long MDF shelf, ¾" thick x 15½" wide, referred to as a 1x16 throughout this plan

Wood glue

1¼" pocket hole screws

1¼" finish nails

2" finish nails (optional)

- **1** set of 16" white Euro-style drawer slides
- **1** knob

Finishing supplies

TOOLS

Basic hand tools

Circular saw or other saw for making crosscuts

Pocket hole jig

Finish nailer

Drill

CUTTING LIST

- **2** 7¼"-long **1x16s** (side aprons)
- **4** 24"-long **2x2s** (legs)
- **6** 16¾"-long **1x2s** (front/ back trim)
- **1** 19¾"-long **1x16** (bottom shelf)
- **1** 23¾"-long **1x16** (center top)
- **1** 23¾"-long **1x2** (top back)
- **1** 23¾"-long **1x4** (top front)
- **1** 19¾" x 8" piece of ¼" plywood (back)
- **2** 17"-long **1x4s** (drawer sides)
- **2** 14¼"-long **1x4s** (drawer ends)
- **1** 17" x 15¾" piece of ¼" plywood (drawer bottom)
- **1** 16½"-long **1x6** (drawer face)

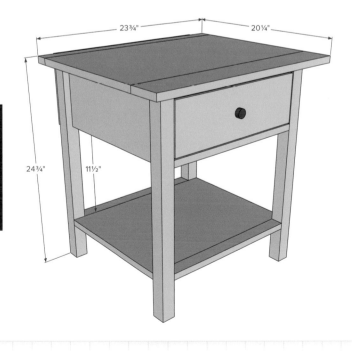

DIMENSIONS

23¾"
20¼"
24¾"
11½"

TIP Check to make sure your 1x6 is a true 5½" (14cm) width; otherwise you will need to adjust the plan for a better-fitting drawer face.

TIP To make a narrower or deeper end table, simply adjust the width of the 1x16 to the desired width. You also can use a 1x12 here for a narrower side table.

① LEGS

Drill ¾" (2cm) pocket holes on both ends of the side aprons, as shown in diagram. Attach legs to side aprons with wood glue and 1¼" (3cm) pocket hole screws.

② FRONT/BACK TRIM

Drill ¾" (2cm) pocket holes on each end of the front and back trim boards as shown in the diagram. Mark the placement and attach with wood glue and 1¼" (3cm) pocket hole screws.

③ BOTTOM SHELF

Drill ¾" (2cm) pocket holes along the long edges of the bottom shelf. Use wood glue and 1¼" (3cm) pocket hole screws to attach shelf to trim and legs.

④ TOP

Build your top as shown in the diagram with ¾" (2cm) pocket holes, keeping top edges flush, use glue and 1¼" (3cm) pocket hole screws. Turn the project upside down and attach the cabinet to the top, using wood glue and 1¼" (3cm) pocket hole screws. Alternatively you can use glue and 1¼" (3cm) finish nails.

⑤ BACK

Attach back to project with wood glue and 2" (5cm) finish nails.

TIP You may attach the back after installing the drawer to give you more room to work.

⑥ DRAWER

Build the drawer as shown in diagram, either with 1¼" (3cm) pocket hole screws set for ¾" (2cm) stock, or using glue and 2" (5cm) finish nails. Attach bottom plywood to drawer bottom with wood glue and 1¼" (3cm) finish nails.

⑦ INSTALL DRAWER

Install drawer in end table with drawer slides. Make sure the drawer box is inset by ¾" (2cm) to allow for the drawer face to be attached in the final step. Check to make sure your drawer slides evenly and smoothly.

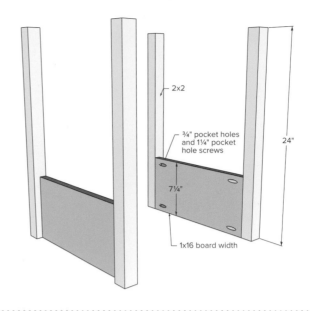

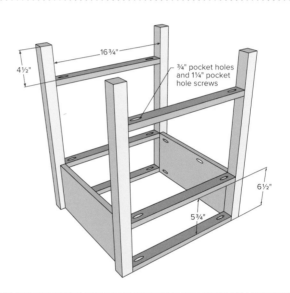

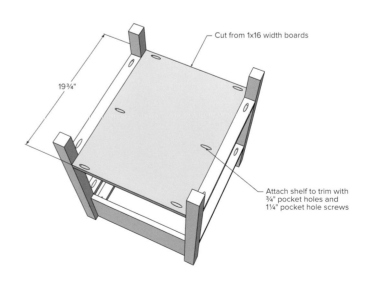

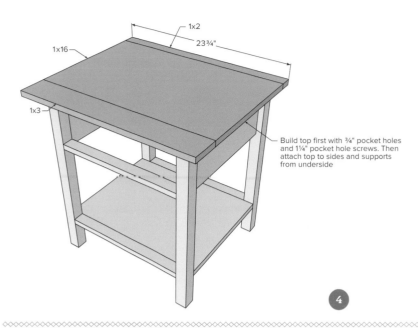

1x2
23¾"
1x16
1x3

Build top first with ¾" pocket holes and 1¼" pocket hole screws. Then attach top to sides and supports from underside

4

8 DRAWER FACE

Once the drawer is installed, push it completely inside the table. Set the face on the drawer box, adjusting until there is an even ⅛" (3mm) gap on all sides. When pleased with the placement, attach the face to the drawer box with glue and 1¼" (3cm) finish nails. Pull the drawer open and attach the face with a few additional 1¼" (3cm) screws from the inside for added strength. Install hardware on drawer face.

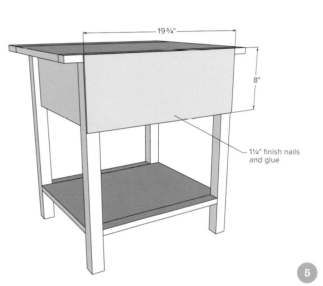

19¾"
8"

1¼" finish nails and glue

5

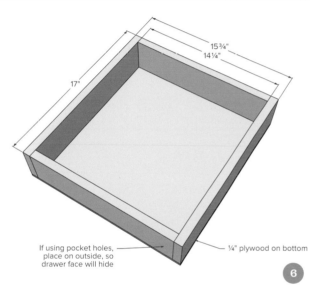

15¾"
14¼"
17"

If using pocket holes, place on outside, so drawer face will hide

¼" plywood on bottom

6

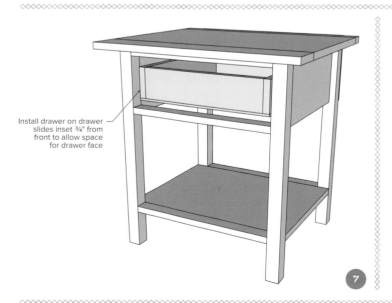

Install drawer on drawer slides inset ¾" from front to allow space for drawer face

7

16½"

Nail drawer face to drawer box with even 1/8" gap on all sides

8

1 BATTING

Start by using the spray adhesive to attach the foam to the plywood, leaving a 2¼" (5.5cm) space empty around all the sides. If you splice the foam from smaller pieces, or if you just want to soften the look of the fabric over the foam, add batting (in the size of the foam) over the foam with the spray adhesive. Then cut your fabric to the size of the plywood and staple on as shown in the diagram.

2 TOP TRIM

Over the stapled-on fabric, attach the top trim with wood glue and 1" (2.5cm) finish nails.

3 SIDE TRIM

Attach the side trim, lining up the outer edges and top trim, with 1" (2.5cm) finish nails.

4 TOP

Keeping the front edge flush, attach the top to the top of headboard. Use wood glue and 2" (5cm) finish nails. The top will overhang the sides by ¾" (2cm).

5 LEGS

Attach the legs to the outsides of headboard with wood glue and 2" (5cm) finish nails. The front edges are flush.

6 BOTTOM SUPPORT

Attach bottom support to the back of the side trim with wood glue and 2" (5cm) finish nails. Attach side molding to bottom support as well. Use bottom support to attach the headboard to the bed frame. Depending on the bed-frame support, you may need to attach the headboard to the wall behind the bed.

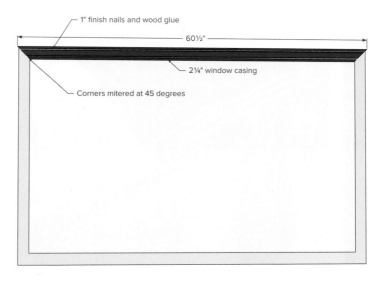

Spray adhesive to attach foam to back plywood. Cover with batting and fabric, stapling fabric to back of plywood

2¼"
56"
37½"
33"
60½"
2¼"
2¼"

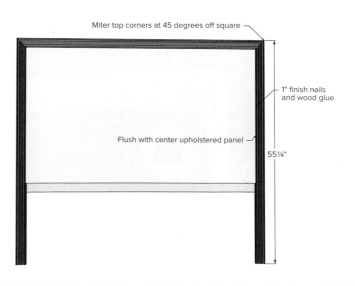

1" finish nails and wood glue
60½"
2¼" window casing
Corners mitered at 45 degrees

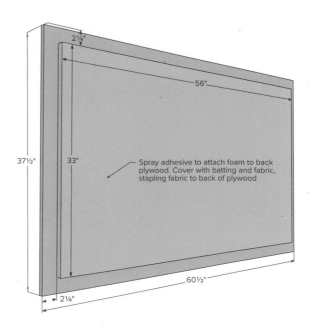

Miter top corners at 45 degrees off square
1" finish nails and wood glue
Flush with center upholstered panel
55¼"

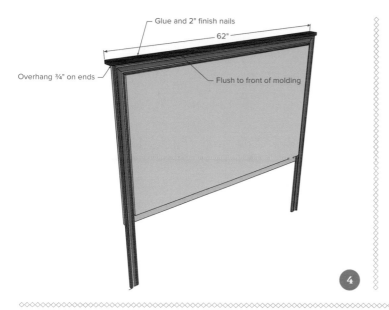

Glue and 2" finish nails

62"

Overhang ¾" on ends

Flush to front of molding

4

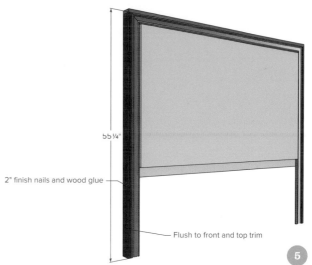

55¼"

2" finish nails and wood glue

Flush to front and top trim

5

Attach with either 1¼" pocket hole screws or
2" countersunk screws and glue. Also attach
from front of legs with 1¼" finish nails and glue

60½"

6

· SHAUNNA & MATT'S TIP ·

To save time, have two pairs of hands available
when you begin adding the foam and fabric to your
headboard. Begin stapling fabric in the corners, having
one person pull the opposite sides tightly while another
person staples the fabric in place. Remember you can
always add or remove staples until the desired look
is achieved! If you would like your headboard to be
a bit taller, don't trim the "legs" until you've placed
it in the room. Then you'll be able to get the perfect
height. Most important, go for it and have fun creating
something beautiful for your home!

PROJECT
Nº 26
ARMOIRE

WITH THIS ARMOIRE, THE GOAL WAS TO
create extra storage for any room of the home
without overwhelming the room. Add style
and storage to your bedroom using this as a
wardrobe or for extra linens, fill up an awkward
corner of a bathroom with towel storage, or
use it in your dining or living space for added
storage. Add extra shelves to create a wine
rack. You could even feature it in a nursery or
office—the uses for this armoire are endless.

Paint the armoire white as Amanda did, or
choose a color or stain to change the look.

SHOPPING LIST

- **2** 8'-long 1x2s
- **4** 8'-long 2x2s
- **1** 4'-long 1x4
- **5** 8'-long 1x3s
- **1** sheet of ¾" plywood, cut into strips 15¾" wide x 8' long (referred to as 1x16s)
- **1** sheet of ¼" plywood

Wood glue

1¼"pocket hole screws

2½" pocket hole screws

2" screws

1¼" finish nails

2" finish nails

- **1** 36" x 30" piece of ¼" acrylic glass
- **1** package mirror clips for ¼" mirror
- **2** sets of 16" Euro-style drawer slides
- **2** sets of surface-mount inset Euro-style hinges
- **4** knobs or handles
- **8** shelf pins (for adjustable shelves, optional)

Stops, clasps, or hatches for closing the doors (optional)

TOOLS

Basic hand tools

Finish nailer

Pocket hole jig

Circular saw or other saw for making crosscuts

Drill

CUTTING LIST

- **2** 15¾"-long **1x2s** (side trim)
- **2** 47¼"-long **1x16s** (sides)
- **4** 51¼"-long **2x2s** (legs)
- **4** 38"-long **2x2s** (top/ bottom trim on front/ back)
- **2** 3¾"-long **1x2s** (center drawer trim)
- **2** 38"-long **1x2s** (drawer bottom trim)
- **1** 6"-long **1x16** (drawer divider)
- **3** 38"-long **1x16s** (shelves)
- **1** 43"-long **1x2** (top back)
- **1** 43"-long **1x16** (top center)
- **1** 43"-long **1x3** (top front)
- **1** 41" x 48" piece of ¼" plywood (back)
- **4** 16"-long **1x3s** (drawer sides)
- **2** 16⅛"-long **1x3s** (drawer backs)
- **2** 17⅝" x 16" pieces of ¼" plywood (drawer bottoms)
- **2** 18⅜"-long **1x4s** (drawer faces)
- **4** 39½"-long **1x3s** (door frames)
- **4** 13¾"-long **1x3s** (door frames)
- **2** 36" x 15" pieces of ¼" acrylic glass (door inserts)

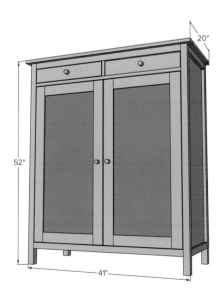

20"

52"

41"

1 SIDE TRIM

Apply glue to the back side of the side trim. Nail with 1¼" (3cm) finish nails to tops and bottoms of sides, with all outside edges flush to the outside.

TIP Drill ¾" (2cm) pocket holes along side edges of sides spaced every 6" to 8" (15cm to 20.5cm) for attaching legs in the next step.

You will need to build two.

2 LEGS

With top edges flush, attach legs to the side panels. Use glue and 1¼" (3cm) pocket hole screws, attaching through ¾" (2cm) pocket holes drilled in previous step.

3 TOP AND BOTTOM TRIM

Drill 1½" (3.8cm) pocket holes on each end of top and bottom trim. Attach to sides, creating the armoire's frame. Use glue and 2½" (6.5cm) pocket hole screws.

4 BOTTOM SHELF

Drill pocket holes along all outside edges of the bottom shelf, spaced every 6" to 8" (15cm to 20.5cm). Attach the shelf inside the frame using wood glue and 1¼" (3cm) pocket hole screws. The top of the shelf is flush with the top of the bottom trim.

5 DRAWER-DIVIDER TRIM

Mark center of top trim as shown in diagram. For drawer divider, attach drawer-divider trim to top trim as shown in diagram, using 1¼" (3cm) pocket hole screws through predrilled ¾" (2cm) pocket holes. This is done on the front and back.

6 DRAWER-BOTTOM TRIM

Drill ¾" (2cm) pocket holes on each end of the drawer-bottom trim. Mark 3¾" (9.5cm) down from top trim, and attach to the sides. Also attach drawer-bottom trim to the drawer-divider trim using glue and 2" (5cm) wood screws through predrilled holes. This is done on the front and back.

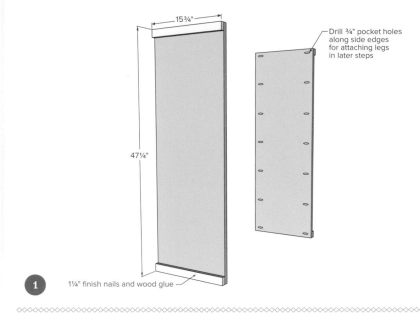

15¾"

47¼"

Drill ¾" pocket holes along side edges for attaching legs in later steps

1 — 1¼" finish nails and wood glue

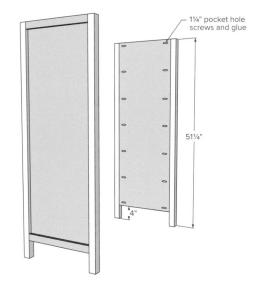

1¼" pocket hole screws and glue

51¼"

4"

2

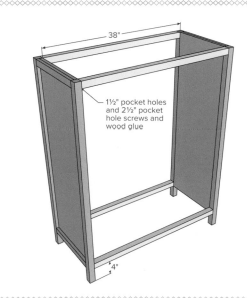

38"

1½" pocket holes and 2½" pocket hole screws and wood glue

4"

3

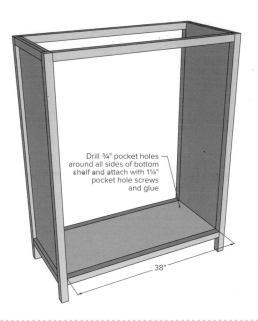
· AMANDA'S TIP ·

"I painted the pieces separately before assembling the armoire."

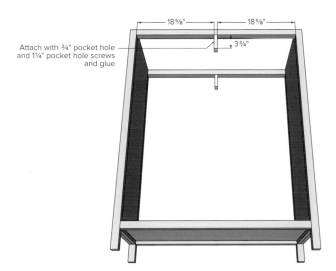

18 ⅝"   18 ⅝"

Attach with ¾" pocket hole and 1¼" pocket hole screws and glue

3¾"

5

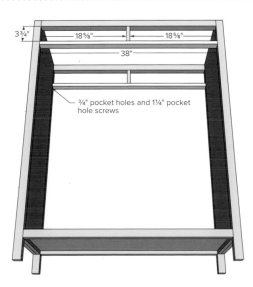

3¾"   18 ⅝"   18 ⅝"

38"

¾" pocket holes and 1¼" pocket hole screws

6

7 DRAWER DIVIDER

Drill pocket holes along the top and side edges of the drawer divider. Attach in place, flush with the drawer-divider trim board. Use wood glue, ¾" (2cm) pocket holes and 1¼" (3cm) pocket hole screws.

8 TOP

Build the top first with ¾" (2cm) pocket holes and 1¼" (3cm) pocket hole screws. Then attach it to the top of the armoire with wood glue and 2" (5cm) finish nails.

9 BACK

Apply glue to all back edges. Lay plywood back on top and nail down with 1¼" (3cm) finish nails.

10 DRAWERS

Build drawers using the specified 1x3s for sides and back, ¼" (6mm) plywood for bottom, and 1x4 for the face. Remember the face covers the bottom of the drawer and extends ⅜" (10mm) on either side of drawer box.

11 SHELVES

Shelves can be fixed by attaching with wood glue and ¾" (2cm) pocket holes and 1¼" (3cm) pocket hole screws; or they can be made adjustable with shelf pins.

12 DOORS

Doors should always be built to fit the door openings. Measure the overall opening size. Divide the width by 2 to figure the overall opening size for each door. Subtract ¼" (6mm) from both height and width to allow even gaps around the inset doors. These measurements are the overall size of the frame. Build the frame using 1x3s, wood glue, and ¾" (2cm) pocket holes with 1¼" (3cm) pocket hole screws. Attach acrylic glass with mirror clips to the inside of each door. Attach the doors to the cabinet with hinges.

TIP Install stops, clasps, or hatches to keep doors in place when closed.

Attach with ¾" pocket holes and 1¼" pocket hole screws and glue

15¾" 6"

7

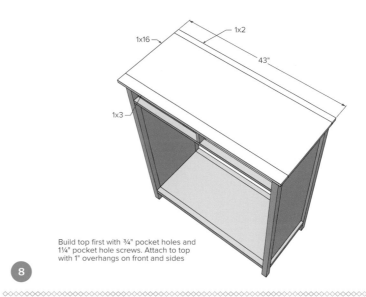

1x16   1x2   43"

1x3

Build top first with ¾" pocket holes and 1¼" pocket hole screws. Attach to top with 1" overhangs on front and sides

8

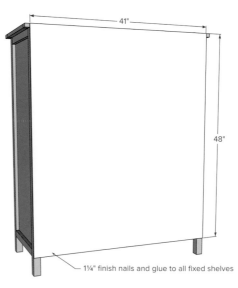

41"

48"

1¼" finish nails and glue to all fixed shelves

9

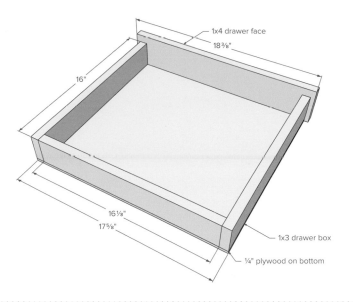

1x4 drawer face

18⅜"

16"

16⅛"

17⅝"

1x3 drawer box

¼" plywood on bottom

10

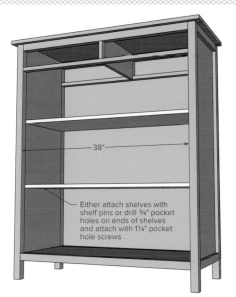

38"

Either attach shelves with shelf pins or drill ¾" pocket holes on ends of shelves and attach with 1¼" pocket hole screws

11

13¾"

39½"

12

9
CHILDREN'S ROOM

BELOW: Play table
and chairs
ABOVE RIGHT:
Play kitchen
BELOW RIGHT:
Bunkbed

There is nothing more gratifying

than building projects for your children. The amazement and delight of having child-sized furniture made with love is only topped when you overhear your child proudly say, "My mama built me this!"

This chapter includes plans for a play kitchen sink and stove, a play table, and a child-sized chair. There's also a very-easy-to-build bunk bed with integrated ladder and side rails that is made mostly of 2x4s! With these projects, you will be able to update your child's room even on a very limited budget.

PLAY TABLE

SHOPPING LIST

1   8'-long 2x2
1   8'-long 1x3s
1   24" x 48" piece of ¾"
    plywood or project panel
Wood glue
1¼" pocket hole screws

TOOLS

Basic hand tools
Finish nailer
Pocket hole jig
Circular saw or other saw for making crosscuts
Drill

CUTTING LIST

4   **20¼"-long 2x2s** (legs)
2   **19"-long 1x3s** (end aprons)
2   **37"-long 1x3s** (side aprons)
1   **24" x 48" piece ¾" plywood or hobby board** (top)

EVERY HOME WITH CHILDREN SHOULD have a durable, kid-size table. And now you can, with this simple plan that even the woodworker novice can tackle. Once you have this conquered, make the matching chairs (page 159)!

Amy built this table and stapled pretty fabric to the inside to create a hidden storage area for craft supplies underneath the table. Leave the table open, or create a little extra storage, as Amy did.

DIMENSIONS

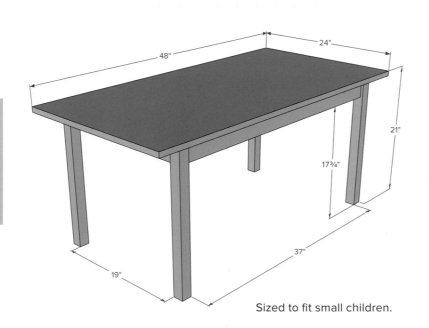

Sized to fit small children.

· BUILT BY ·
AMY HUNTLEY
www.theidearoom.net

"This is a perfect table for kids to craft on or to play on. Not too big and not too small."

Build the chairs too, go to page 159.

1 END APRONS

Drill ¾" (2cm) pocket holes on each end of each apron. Also drill ¾" (2cm) pocket holes along the top edge for attaching the tabletop in later steps. Attach the end aprons to the legs, centering end aprons on the legs, with 1¼" (3cm) pocket hole screws.

2 SIDE APRONS

Drill ¾" (2cm) pocket holes on each end of each side apron. Also drill ¾" (2cm) pocket holes along top edge of side aprons for attaching the tabletop in the final step. Attach side aprons to legs with glue and 1¼" (3cm) pocket hole screws.

3 TABLETOP

Mark underside of tabletop 4" (10cm) from each end and 1" (2.5cm) from each side. Line the table base up with the marks, and attach through the predrilled pocket holes with glue and 1¼" (3cm) pocket hole screws.

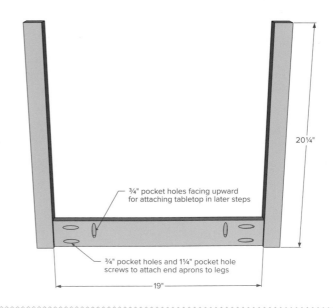

20¼"

¾" pocket holes facing upward for attaching tabletop in later steps

¾" pocket holes and 1¼" pocket hole screws to attach end aprons to legs

19"

1

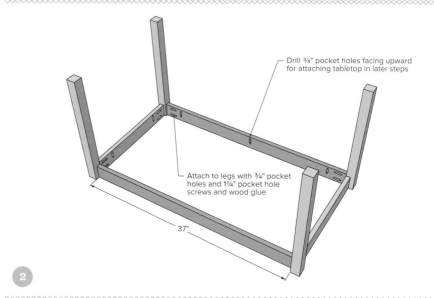

Drill ¾" pocket holes facing upward for attaching tabletop in later steps

Attach to legs with ¾" pocket holes and 1¼" pocket hole screws and wood glue

37"

2

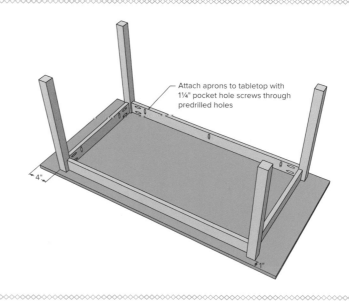

Attach aprons to tabletop with 1¼" pocket hole screws through predrilled holes

4"

1"

3

PROJECT
Nº 28

CHILDREN'S CHAIR

CHAIRS LIKE THESE WERE USED BY MY daughter from her youngest toddler years, through preschool, and even into grade school. She loves having her own chair. My husband and I have also used this chair to reach a top shelf or change a lightbulb.

For the book, I've updated the plans to be easier to build and use fewer materials. Amy built these chairs. We decided to add the back cutout handle, but you can choose not to do the extra work.

SHOPPING LIST

- 2   8'-long 2x2s
- 1   24"-long 1x4
- 1   8'-long 1x2
- 1   16"-long 1x12
- Wood glue
- 1¼" pocket hole screws
- 2½" pocket hole screws
- 1¼" finish nails

TOOLS

- Basic hand tools
- Drill
- Jigsaw
- Pocket hole jig
- Finish nailer
- Circular saw or other saw for making crosscuts
- Finishing tools

CUTTING LIST

- 2   26½"-long **2x2s** (back legs)
- 2   12½"-long **2x2s** (front legs)
- 1   12"-long **1x4s** (back)
- 1   12"-long **2x2** (back support)
- 3   12"-long **1x2s** (front apron)
- 4   9¾"-long **1x2s** (supports)
- 1   12¾"-long **1x2** (bottom support)
- 1   15"-long **1x12** (seat)

DIMENSIONS

15"

13¼"

11¼"

26½"

13¼"

1 BACK

The back cutout is mostly decorative and not necessary for the function of the chair. But adding these extra touches can make your furniture a little more personal. If you choose to add the back cutout, drill holes with a 1" (2.5cm) drill bit centered on the 1x4 back, 4" (10cm) from outside edges. Then connect the holes by cutting them out with a jigsaw. Round the corners with an elongated arch cut.

TIP Draw one half of the arch shape and cut out. Use the scrap as a pattern for cutting remaining arches.

Drill ¾" (2cm) pocket holes along both ends on all back boards, excluding legs. Attach all back boards to legs with 1¼" (3cm) pocket hole screws and glue.

2 FRONT

Drill ¾" (2cm) pocket holes on each end of the front apron. Attach with glue and 1¼" (3cm) pocket hole screws to the tops of the front legs, with tops flush and the front apron centered on the front legs.

TIP To hide screw holes when attaching the seat, consider drilling ¾" (2cm) pocket holes facing upward in all aprons.

3 CHAIR FRAME

Drill ¾" (2cm) pocket holes on each end of the side aprons. Attach the side aprons to the back using 1¼" (3cm) pocket hole screws, lining them up with the back support. Then attach the front to the side aprons to complete the chair frame.

4 BOTTOM SUPPORTS

Add bottom supports by drilling ¾" (2cm) pocket holes on each end of each board. Then attach them in place, centering the side supports on the legs and centering the center support on the side supports. Use glue and 1¼" (3cm) pocket hole screws.

5 CHAIR SEAT

Use wood glue and 1¼" (3cm) finish nails to attach the chair seat to the chair frame. Nail the seat into all legs and aprons for the strongest fit. (**Note:** If you predrilled pocket holes, simply attach the seat with 1¼" [3cm] pocket hole screws and glue.)

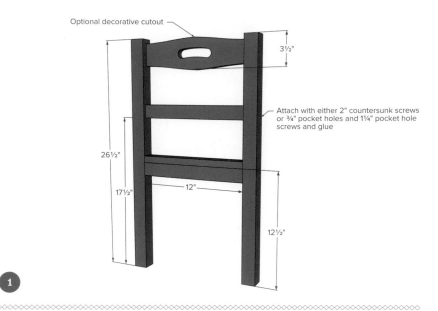

Optional decorative cutout

Attach with either 2" countersunk screws or ¾" pocket holes and 1¼" pocket hole screws and glue

3½"

26½"

17½"

12"

12½"

1

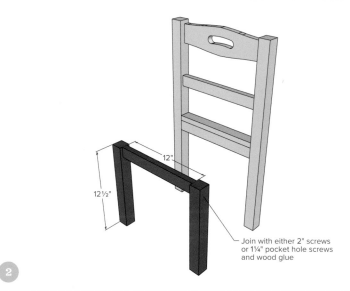

12"

12½"

Join with either 2" screws or 1¼" pocket hole screws and wood glue

2

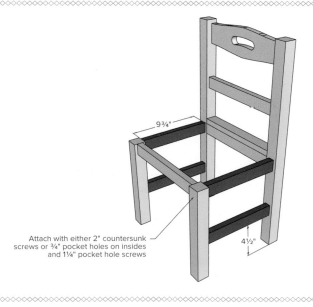

9¾"

4½"

Attach with either 2" countersunk screws or ¾" pocket holes on insides and 1¼" pocket hole screws

3

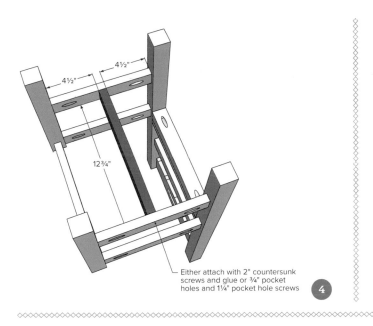

4½"   4½"
4½"
12¾"

Either attach with 2" countersunk
screws and glue or ¾" pocket
holes and 1¼" pocket hole screws

4

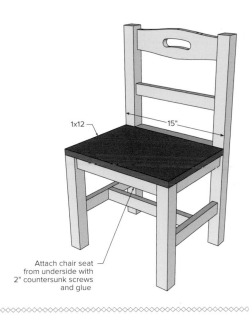

1x12   15"

Attach chair seat
from underside with
2" countersunk screws
and glue

5

· BUILT BY ·
AMY HUNTLEY

" The chairs are a fun and simple design
with the perfect sturdiness for kids. "

PLAY KITCHEN

EVERY NIGHT FOR FOUR DAYS, I SNUCK OUT of bed after my daughter fell asleep to work on this play kitchen for her second birthday. When she pulled the wrapping paper off her present, I felt so much pride and excitement, and I knew that the sacrifice of sleep and a little "me" time was well worth it. She played with that kitchen for years, and I still feel a sense of happiness looking at it.

But my simple play kitchen design took a new turn when Kirsten built it, painting it a beautiful shade of turquoise and adding a hand-sewn skirt for the sink. Even as the mother of four, Kirsten found time to make what is sure to become a family heirloom.

SHOPPING LIST

- 1   6'-long 1x12
- 1   2'-long 1x10
- 1   12'-long 1x2
- 1   8'-long 1x3
- ¼   sheet of ¼" plywood or hardboard
- Wood glue
- 1¼" finish nails
- 2" finish nails
- 1¼" pocket holes screws (stove only)
- Knobs and pulls as desired
- 1   6"-diameter stainless steel bowl, with lip (sink only)
- 1   set surface-mount inset Euro-style hinges (stove only)
- 9¾" x 11½" x ¼"-thick acrylic glass (stove only) and cutter
- Multisurface adhesive or one package mirror clips (for stove door, optional)

TOOLS

- Basic hand tools
- Finish nailer
- Safety equipment
- Pocket hole jig (for stove only)
- Drill (for stove only)
- Circular saw or other saw for making crosscuts

CUTTING LIST FOR 1

- 2   19½"-long 1x12s (sides)
- 1   13"-long 1x12 (bottom shelf)
- 1   13"-long 1x2 (footer)
- 1   13"-long 1x3 (header)
- 1   14½"-long 1x12 (countertop)
- 1   14½"- long 1x3 (backsplash)
- 1   13"-long 1x10 (shelf)
- 1   14½" x 20¼" piece of ¼" plywood or hardboard (back)

STOVE ACCESSORIES

- 2   12¾"-long 1x3s (stove door)
- 2   9½"-long 1x3s (stove door)
- 1   9¾" x 11½" piece of ¼" acrylic glass

DIMENSIONS

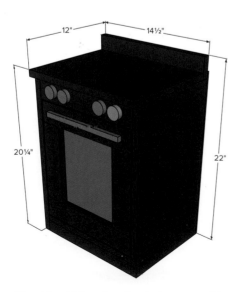

12"   14½"   20¼"   22"

Sized for children from two to ten years old.

The matching refrigerator is DIY too!
Visit ana-white.com for the plans.

1   BOTTOM SHELF

Mark the sides 1½" (3.8cm) from the bottom. Attach the bottom shelf to the sides, with a 1½" (3.8cm) space under the bottom shelf, using wood glue and 2" (5cm) finish nails.

2   FOOTER

Apply glue to the top and side edges of the footer. Set inset, approximately ¼" (6mm) under the bottom shelf, and attach with glue and 2" (5cm) finish nails from the sides and top.

3   HEADER

Apply glue to the ends of the header. Nail in place at the project's front top, using 2" (5cm) finish nails.

4   COUNTERTOP

Attach the backsplash to the countertop with wood glue and 2" (5cm) finish nails.

5   ASSEMBLY

Attach the countertop to the base with wood glue and 2" (5cm) finish nails.

6   SHELF

Mark the shelf's placement by measuring 9¼" (23.5cm) up from the bottom of the project. Attach the shelf, flush to the back, with wood glue and 2" (5cm) finish nails.

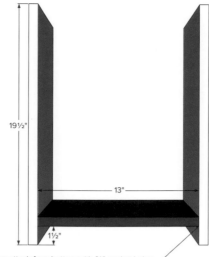

19½"

13"

1½"

Either attach from bottom with ¾" pocket holes and 1¼" pocket hole screws or 2" countersunk screws or nails from outside with glue

1

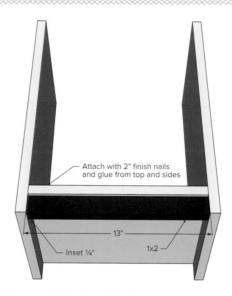

Attach with 2" finish nails and glue from top and sides

13"

Inset ¼"

1x2

2

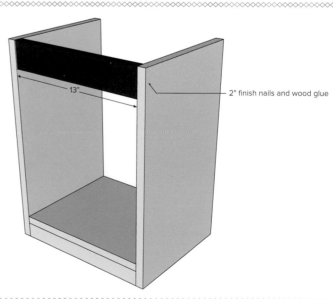

13"

2" finish nails and wood glue

3

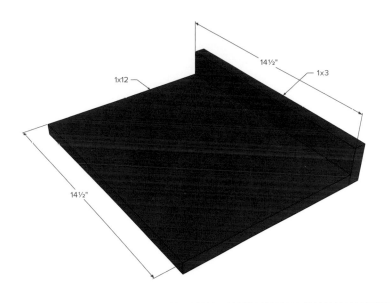

14½"

1x12

1x3

14½"

4

2" finish nails and wood glue

#537

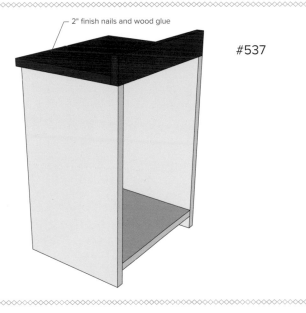

5

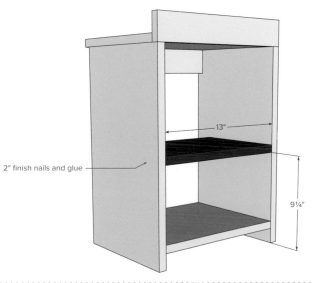

2" finish nails and glue

13"

9¼"

6

7 BACK

Apply glue to all back edges and place the plywood on the back. Nail down with 1¼" (3cm) finish nails.

8 SINK (OPTIONAL)

For the sink, place the metal bowl facedown on the countertop. Trace. With the jigsaw, cut out a hole slightly smaller than the traced shape, testing the fit of the metal bowl. Remember, you can always cut more wood out, but it is very difficult to repair the countertop if you over-cut. When the bowl fits properly, with the lip flush with the countertop, apply adhesive and glue down the bowl. Add the faucet and other accessories to create a sink.

9 STOVE DOOR (OPTIONAL)

Build the stove door from a 1x3 frame, drilling two pocket holes in the frame board ends. Attach to build the stove door frame with wood glue and 1¼" (3cm) pocket hole screws.

10 GLASS DOOR (OPTIONAL)

Cut acrylic glass to size if necessary. Either attach with adhesive or use mirror clips to hold the acrylic glass in place.

11 STOVE-DOOR INSTALLATION

Install the completed stove door with hinges so that the stove door has an even ⅛" (3mm) gap around all edges. The stove door may require installation of a clasp to keep the door shut.

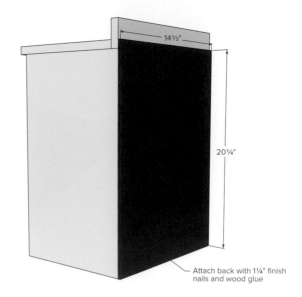

14½"

20¼"

Attach back with 1¼" finish nails and wood glue

7

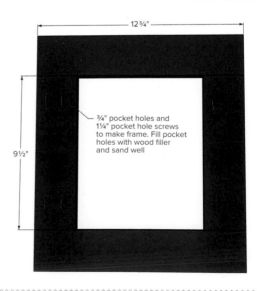

For sink, trace top of metal bowl on top for sink. Cut out slightly smaller so lip holds sink in place

8

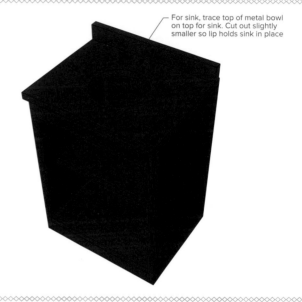

12¾"

9½"

¾" pocket holes and 1¼" pocket hole screws to make frame. Fill pocket holes with wood filler and sand well

9

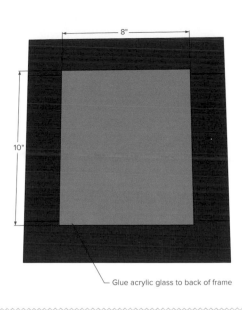

10"   8"

Glue acrylic glass to back of frame ⑩

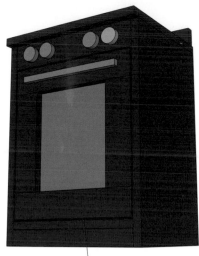

Attach door with hinges so there is an even
⅛" gap around all sides of the door ⑪

· KIRSTEN'S SINK SKIRT: QUICK CURTAIN MINITUTORIAL ·

This sink skirt is easy to make. The ruffles are sewn to a heavier-duty fabric, so it hangs straight. The dimensions of the fabric pieces (before any sewing) are as follows: Main heavier-duty fabric piece: 15½" (39.5cm) wide x 17½" (44.5cm) long with ½" (13mm) seam allowances. The circumference of the loop at the top is 4" (10cm) with a ½" (13mm) seam allowance.

The colorful fabric at the top was sewn on after the three ruffles and about ½" (13mm) over the top of the pink ruffle.

The dimensions of each ruffle before sewing: 10½" (26.5cm) x 22" (56cm).

To sew each ruffle, put the fabric backside down and horizontal; bring the bottom up so that the colorful sides are together, and sew with a ¼" (6mm) seam allowance. Turn inside out, and then sew again along the top; the ends are still open and now you have a long tube.

Fold the ends in, and sew the ends closed.

To prepare for gathering the fabric, make two rows of basting stitches (long stitches) ¼" (6mm) from the top and about ¼" (6mm) apart, and leave long tails of thread on each end. After you do this, pull the thread lightly until the fabric gathers evenly. Then pin the ruffle to the main piece, and sew a regular stitch between the two basting stitches. Pull the basting stitches out after it is properly sewn in place, leaving the regular stitching line—slick!

The bottom of each ruffle hangs about ¾" (2cm) over the ruffle beneath it. The fabric over the loop (white-, green-, blue-colored) is sewn over the pink ruffle about ½" (13mm). The blue pom-pom row is sewn right where the top of the pink fabric and the colorful loop fabric join. The bottom ruffle hangs about 1" (2.5cm) below the main piece of fabric. The edges and bottom of each ruffle hang free. Whew—that was probably a little confusing. Got it?

· BUILT BY ·
REBECCA RIDNER
BeccaDaleDesigns.com

PROJECT
Nº 30

BUNK BED

SHOPPING LIST

11 10'-long 2x4s
4 8'-long 2x2s
2 8'-long 1x3s
Wood glue
2½" pocket hole screws
2" screws
Bunkie boards or 39"-long 1x3s for slats, per mattress manufacturer recommendations

TOOLS

Basic hand tools
Pocket hole jig
Circular saw or other saw for making crosscuts
Drill

CUTTING LIST

10 36"-long **2x4s** (end rails)
4 62"-long **2x4s** (legs)
6 75"-long **2x4s** (side rails)
4 75"-long **2x2s** (cleats)
1 52"-long **1x3** (ladder side)
2 60"-long **2x4s** (front guardrail)
3 16½"-long **1x3s** (guardrail supports)
2 17½"-long **1x3s** (ladder rungs)

WHEN I STARTED DESIGNING THIS BUNK BED plan, I really wanted to focus on simplicity, affordability, and easy construction. With an integrated ladder and guardrails, this bunk bed has it all. Paint it a bright color like Rebecca did for maximum impact, or choose a natural wood stain for a cozy cabin feel.

DIMENSIONS

Fits standard 39" x 75" (99cm x 191cm) twin mattresses.

1 ENDS

Drill two 1½" (3.8cm) pocket holes on each end of each end-rail board. Mark all four legs as shown in the diagram. Use glue and 2½" (6.5cm) pocket hole screws to attach the end-rail boards to the legs. Adjust for square. Build two.

2 SIDE RAILS

Drill two 1½" (3.8cm) pocket holes on each end of each side-rail board. Attach with 2½" (6.5cm) pocket hole screws to each end of the bunk bed to create the frame of the bunk bed. Do not use glue here so that the bed can be disassembled easily.

3 CLEATS

Screw the cleats to the side rails and legs with 2" (5cm) screws, matching diagram placement.

4 LADDER SIDE

Measure and mark the location of the ladder side board. Glue and screw the ladder side board, through predrilled holes with 2" (5cm) screws, to the side rails on the front.

5 FRONT GUARDRAIL

Drill two 1½" (3.8cm) pocket holes on one end of each front guardrail. Attach to the legs with 2½" (6.5cm) pocket hole screws. Then attach to the ladder side board with 2" (5cm) predrilled screws.

6 GUARDRAIL TRIM

Measure and mark the location of the guardrail trim on the guardrails. Predrill holes for 2" (5cm) wood screws, and attach the guardrail trim to the guardrails using glue and 2" (5cm) screws. Add ladder rungs with 2" (5cm) screws and glue.

7 SLATS OR BUNKIE BOARD

Use either a bunkie board or slat system to hold each mattress in place. If using slats, cut enough slats to meet the specifications of the mattress, and screw them down securely. For most twin mattresses, fourteen slats are necessary.

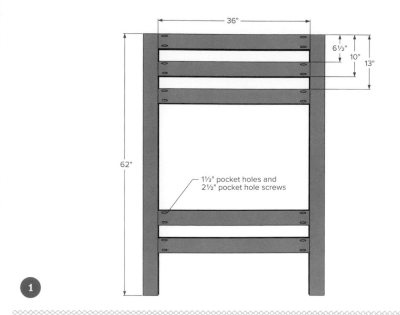

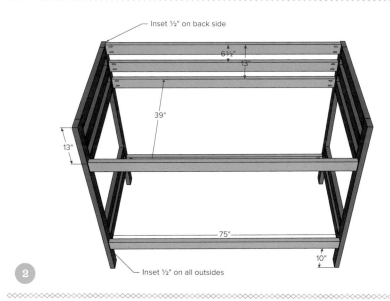

59"
16½"
52"
15"
2" screws and glue

4

57½"
1½" pocket holes and 2½" pocket hole screws
2" screws and glue

5

16½"
16½"
16½"
16½"
2" screws and glue
20½"
17½"
9"

6

You can use a slat system in place of bunkie board. Follow recommendations from mattress manufacturer for slat spacing and strength requirements

Mattress must NOT be more than 5" from top of top guardrails on top bunk

7

10

OUTDOOR FURNISHINGS

I am very excited about the outdoor

projects in this chapter. For the Adirondack chairs, I spent months considering how to simplify the classic Adirondack chair, without sacrificing comfort or quality. Though they are easy and inexpensive to build, I know you will love the comfort and styling of my new Adirondack chairs. And no patio or backyard would be complete without sturdy benches and a picnic table.

TOP LEFT: Dining table and bench
BOTTOM ROW: Children and adult
Adirondack chairs

ADULT ADIRONDACK CHAIR

SHOPPING LIST

6 8'-long 1x4s
1 8'-long 1x2
1¼" and 2" wood screws

TOOLS

Basic hand tools
Compound miter saw
Drill with countersink drill bits
Finish nailer
Jigsaw

CUTTING LIST

2 23¼"-long **1x2s** (arm supports)
2 23¾"-long **1x4s** (front legs)
2 24⅝"-long **1x4s**, both ends cut at 15 degrees off square, ends *are* parallel (back legs)
2 26⅜"-long **1x4s**, longest measurement, ends cut in same direction, 20 degrees off square and 5 degrees off square (stringers)
6 21"-long **1x4s** (front apron and seat slats)
5 33"-long **1x4s** (back slats)
2 19½"-long **1x2s** (back supports)
1 19½"-long **1x4** (back base)
2 23¼"-long **1x4s** (armrests)

IN MY TIME, I'VE MADE QUITE A FEW
Adirondack chairs. I've loved them all. But this one I love the most. With this design, the same styling and comfort we all love in an Adirondack chair is apparent. But by adding back legs, these chairs are more compact and less expensive to build. They are also easier to build, requiring only straight-angle cuts.

Once you make one, you will find yourself wanting to make tons. You have been warned!

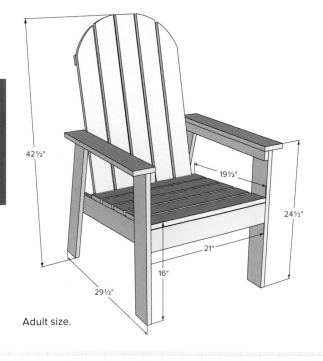

DIMENSIONS

42½"
19½"
24½"
21"
16"
29½"

Adult size.

1 LEGS AND ARM SUPPORT

Before we get started on the legs, consider that your two leg sets will need to be built mirrored so that the arm support is on the inside of each leg set. If you forget, no biggie—you will just be building two chairs!

Lay out one front and one back leg on your work surface. Position the arm support over the tops of the legs and stringers in place so that your legs are positioned at the correct angle. Mark the position of the arm support on the leg tops, and apply glue within the marked areas. Attach with predrilled holes and 1¼" (3cm) screws and glue.

2 STRINGER

The trickiest part of the stringer is getting it cut. Just remember that the angles are in the same direction for each end, though different. And use the measurements to guide you in cutting the measurements correctly.

Mark the front leg in ¾"(2cm) and also 11¾" (30cm) from the bottom of the front leg. Then mark the back leg 9¾" (25cm) up from the bottom of the back leg along the back edge. Fit the stringer, marking its placement on the legs. Apply glue within the marked areas, and replace the stringer. Attach with 1¼" (3cm) screws, predrilled.

3 FRONT APRON

Apply glue to the ends of the front stringer and the ends of the front apron. Attach to the legs and stringers with 2" (5cm) countersunk screws.

4 SEAT SLATS

Starting at the front aprons, attach the seat slats to the stringer with 2" (5cm) predrilled screws and glue. Leave a ½" (13mm) gap between each seat slat.

5 BACK

Lay out the back-slat boards on your work surface. Keep a ½" (13mm) gap between all slats. Adjust to make sure your slats are square by measuring diagonally from opposite outside corners. Attach base support and back supports as noted in diagram.

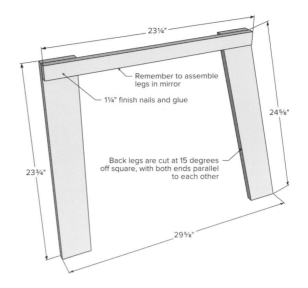

1

23¼"

Remember to assemble legs in mirror

1¼" finish nails and glue

24⅝"

23¾"

Back legs are cut at 15 degrees off square, with both ends parallel to each other

29⅝"

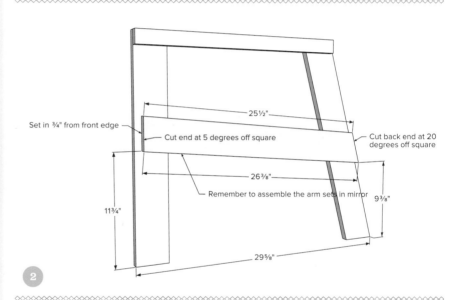

2

Set in ¾" from front edge

25½"

Cut end at 5 degrees off square

Cut back end at 20 degrees off square

26⅜"

Remember to assemble the arm sets in mirror

9⅜"

11¾"

29⅝"

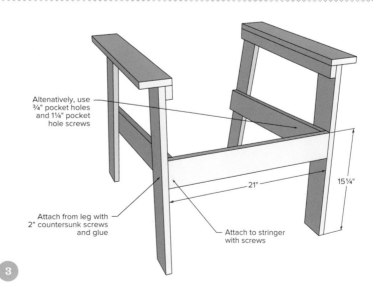

3

Alternatively, use ¾" pocket holes and 1¼" pocket hole screws

Attach from leg with 2" countersunk screws and glue

Attach to stringer with screws

21"

15¼"

2" countersunk screws and wood glue

21"

½" space between seat slats

4

6 BACK ASSEMBLY

Fit the back into the seat of the chair, lining up the base support with the bottom of the stringers. Line the middle back support up with the arm supports. Mark the location and remove, and apply glue within the marked areas. Replace the back, and predrill holes for 2" (5cm) screws through the stringers and arm supports into the back. Attach with 2" (5cm) screws.

7 ARMS

For the finishing touch, apply glue to the tops of the arm supports and leg tops. Place the arms on top, flush to the inside of the arm supports. Screw down with 2" (5cm) countersunk screws.

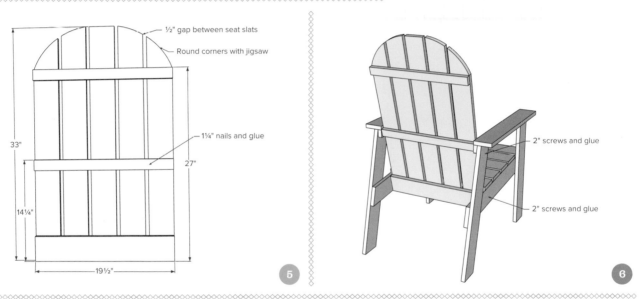

½" gap between seat slats

Round corners with jigsaw

33"

27"

1¼" nails and glue

14¼"

19½"

5

2" screws and glue

2" screws and glue

6

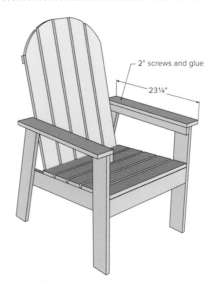

2" screws and glue

23¼"

7

Each chair cost me only
$5 in lumber to make!

CHILDREN'S ADIRONDACK CHAIR

SHOPPING LIST

- 5 8'-long 1x3s
- 1 8'-long 1x2
- 1¼" finish nails
- 1¼" screws
- 2" screws
- Wood glue
- Finishing supplies

TOOLS

- Basic hand tools
- Compound miter saw
- Drill with countersink drill bits
- Finish nailer
- Jigsaw

CUTTING LIST

- 2 18"-long **1x2s** (top armrest supports)
- 2 18"-long **1x3s** (front legs)
- 2 18"-long **1x3s** (armrests)
- 2 18⅝"-long **1x3s**, cut both ends at 15 degrees off square, both ends parallel to each other (back legs)
- 2 20½"-long **1x3s**, front cut at 5 degrees off square, back cut at 20 degrees off square, angles cut in same direction, not parallel (stringers)
- 6 16"-long **1x3s** (front apron and seat boards)
- 5 24"-long **1x3s** (seat backs)
- 2 14½"-long **1x2s** (back supports)
- 1 14½"-long **1x3** (back base support)

HAVING YOUR OWN CHAIR PAINTED A

bright summery color when you are still a toddler is no longer a luxury. Any child can now have his or her very own supercomfy, wooden Adirondack chair. This easy-to-build chair is inexpensive and quick to make. I made all four in a day and spray-painted each a different bright color for each child.

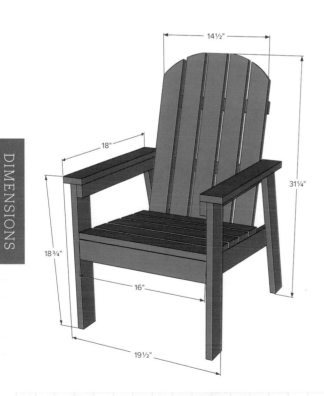

DIMENSIONS

This chair can also be constructed primarily with ¾" (2cm) pocket holes and 1¼" (3cm) pocket hole screws. Just plan out all pocket holes and drill before assembly.

1 TOP ARMREST SUPPORT

Attach the top armrest support to the front and back legs using wood glue and 1¼" (3cm) screws or finish nails. Build two of these, in mirror, with the arm supports on the insides.

2 STRINGER

Mark the location of the stringer on the insides of both back and front legs. Attach the stringer with glue and 1¼" (3cm) finish nails or screws.

3 FRONT APRON

With both leg sides constructed, attach the front apron to both stringers and legs using glue and 2" (5cm) wood screws. Alternatively, ¾" (2cm) pocket holes and 1¼" (3cm) pocket hole screws can be used.

4 SEAT BOARDS

Space the seat boards ½" (13mm) apart, gluing and then screwing or nailing them down with 2" (5cm) fasteners.

5 SEAT BACK

Lay the seat-back boards facedown, spaced ½" (13mm) apart. Attach a bottom support to the base of the seat boards with glue and 1¼" (3cm) finish nails. Mark 9" (23cm) from the base and attach the middle support. Mark 5½" (14cm) from the top and attach top support board with wood glue and 1¼" (3cm) finish nails.

6 ROUNDED CORNERS

For a softer look, use a jigsaw to round the top corners of the seat back. Sand all cuts made with a jigsaw.

7 ASSEMBLY

Fit the seat back in the chair, lining up the middle support with the arms and the base support with the stringers. Screw in place with predrilled 2" (5cm) holes and countersunk screws.

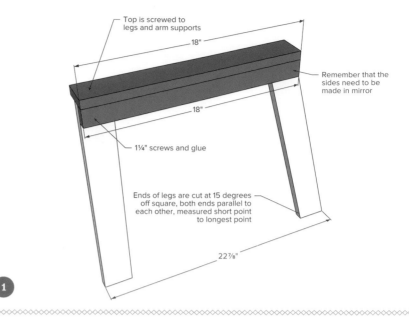

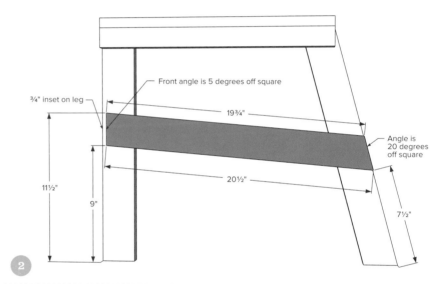

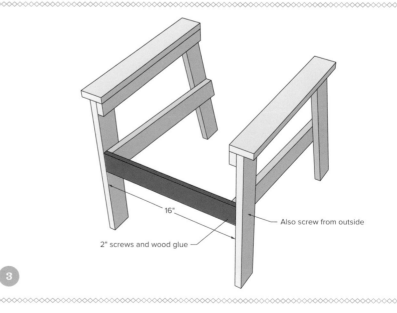

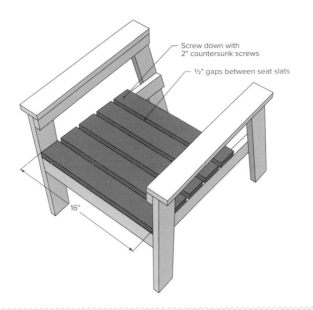

Screw down with
2" countersunk screws

½" gaps between seat slats

16"

4

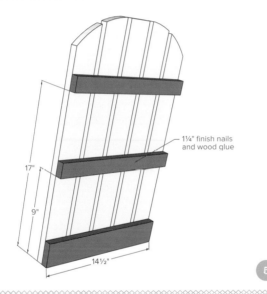

1¼" finish nails
and wood glue

17"

9"

14½"

5

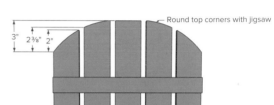

Round top corners with jigsaw

3"   2 ⅜" 2"

6

2" wood screws and glue

7

PICNIC TABLE

SHOPPING LIST

1   **6'-long 1x6**

11 **6'-long 1x4s**

Wood glue

1¼" pocket hole screws

1¼" finish nails

2¾" screws

TOOLS

Pocket hole jig

Drill

Countersink bit

Finish nailer

Miter saw

CUTTING LIST

9   **63"-long 1x4s** (tabletop boards)

2   **33½"-long 1x6s** (breadboard ends)

4   **31½"-long 2x2s** (longest point measurement), both ends cut at **45 degrees** off square, ends are *not* parallel to each other (under-tabletop supports)

4   **41⅜"-long 1x4s** (long point to long point measurement), both ends cut at **45 degrees** off square, ends parallel to each other (leg full pieces)

4   **21⅝"-long 1x4s** (longest point measurement), one end cut at **45 degrees** off square (leg fill-in pieces)

4   **19¾"-long 1x4s** (longest point measurement), one end cut at **45 degrees** off square (leg fill-in pieces)

2   **22¼"-long 1x4s** (longest point measurement), both ends cut at **45 degrees** off square, ends are *not* parallel to each other (under-table angle supports)

I LOVE THE ADDED CHARACTER OF THE X legs, but they are also practical because they make the table more stable. This table has added angle bracing to support the center of the table.

DIMENSIONS

Both ends are cut at 45 degrees off square

22¼"

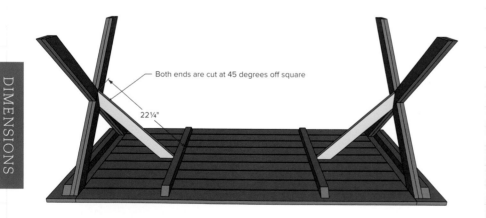

Full-size picnic table.

· BUILT BY ·
LYDIA MANDERS

"I love the simple stylish design of this table, and it draws many compliments. The cross legs make it easy for a guest to slide in and out. And the benches (page 186) complement the table beautifully."

1 TABLETOP

Drill two ¾" (2cm) pocket holes on each end of each 1x4 tabletop board. Spacing the boards ¼" (6mm) apart, attach them to the breadboard ends with wood glue and 1¼" (3cm) pocket hole screws.

2 TABLETOP SUPPORTS

On the underside of the tabletop, mark the location of all the table-base boards. Predrill holes for 2" (5cm) screws in the supports and attach to the tabletop underside at the locations specified in diagrams.

3 LEGS

Lay all legs down parallel so that the ends match. Then position the partial leg pieces as shown in the diagram; glue and nail them down with 1¼" (3cm) finish nails.

4 LEG ASSEMBLY

Match two leg pieces to create the X legs, as shown in diagram. Glue and use four 1¼" (3cm) finish nails to secure the legs where they cross.

5 ATTACHING LEGS TO TABLE BASE

With the wider end positioned away from the tabletop, attach the narrower end of the X bases to the inside of the table supports, using wood glue and 2¾" (7cm) screws through countersunk screw holes.

6 ANGLE SUPPORT

Drill two ¾" (2cm) pocket holes on each angled end of the angle supports. Attach the supports to the underside of the table and to the center of the X legs with wood glue and 1¼" (3cm) pocket hole screws.

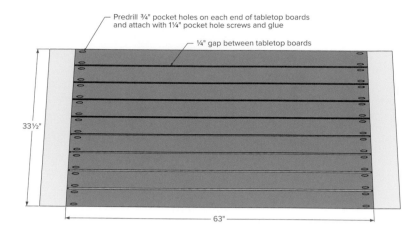

Predrill ¾" pocket holes on each end of tabletop boards and attach with 1¼" pocket hole screws and glue

¼" gap between tabletop boards

33½"

63"

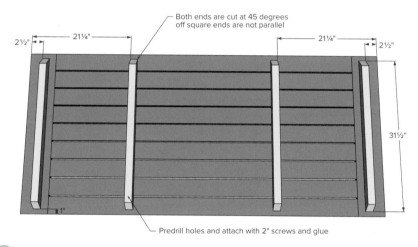

Both ends are cut at 45 degrees off square ends are not parallel

2½"   21¼"   21¼"   2½"

31½"

1"

Predrill holes and attach with 2" screws and glue

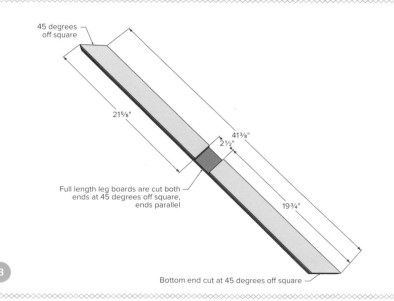

45 degrees off square

21⅝"

41⅜"

2½"

Full length leg boards are cut both ends at 45 degrees off square, ends parallel

19¾"

Bottom end cut at 45 degrees off square

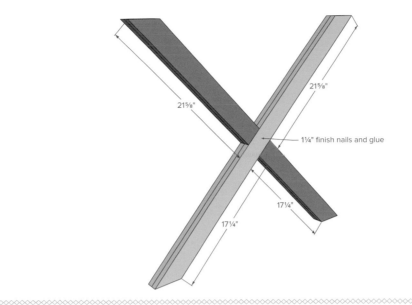

21⅝"

21⅝"

1¼" finish nails and glue

17¼"

17¼"

4

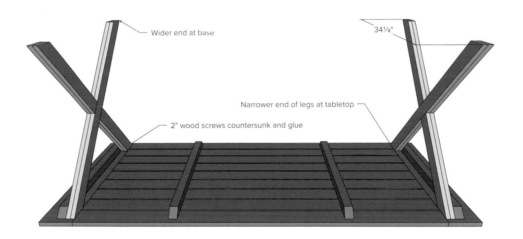

Wider end at base

34⅛"

Narrower end of legs at tabletop

2" wood screws countersunk and glue

5

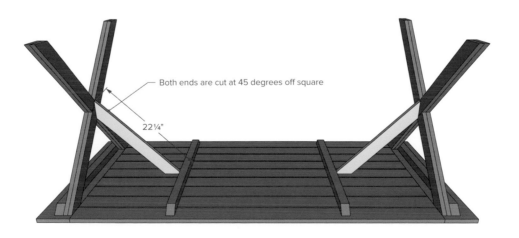

Both ends are cut at 45 degrees off square

22¼"

6

PICNIC BENCH

TO MATCH OUR X TABLE, OF COURSE
we need X benches. These benches have a classic bench feel, but they are sturdy and strong. The three sets of legs support the weight of adults and add a nice touch to the bench.

SHOPPING LIST

- 4   6'-long **1x4s**
- 1   3'-long **1x6**
- 2   8'-long **2x2s**
- 4   8'-long **1x3s**
- Wood glue
- 1¼" pocket hole screws
- 2" screws
- 2¾" screws
- 1¼" finish nails
- Finishing supplies

TOOLS

- Pocket hole jig
- Drill
- Countersink bit
- Finish nailer
- Miter saw

CUTTING LIST

- **4**   62½"-long **1x4s** (bench-top boards)
- **2**   14¾"-long **1x6s** (bench-top breadboard ends)
- **8**   13½"-long **2x2s** (longest point measurement), both ends cut at 30 degrees off square, ends not parallel to each other (under-seat supports)
- **6**   19⅞"-long **1x3s** (long point to short point measurement), both ends cut at 30 degrees off square, ends parallel to each other (full leg pieces)
- **6**   11"-long **1x3s** (longest point measurement), both ends cut at 30 degrees off square, ends not parallel to each other (longer leg fill-in pieces)
- **6**   8⅞"-long **1x3s** (longest point measurement), both ends cut at 30 degrees off square, ends not parallel to each other (shorter leg fill-in pieces)
- **4**   16¾"- long **1x3s** (longest point measurement), one end cut at 30 degrees off square, other end cut at 60 degrees off square, ends not parallel (under-bench angle supports)

DIMENSIONS

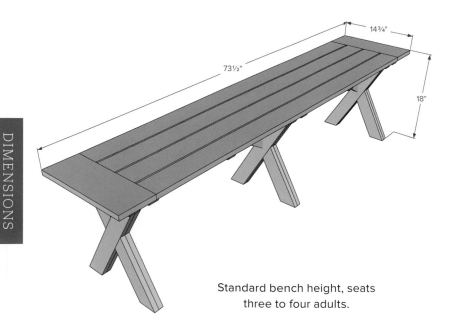

73½"

14¾"

18"

Standard bench height, seats three to four adults.

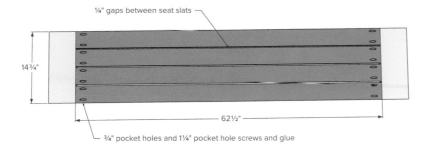

¼" gaps between seat slats

14¾"

62½"

¾" pocket holes and 1¼" pocket hole screws and glue

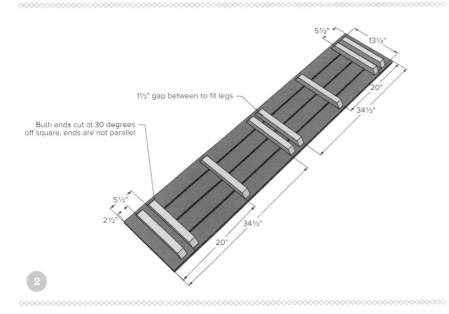

5½"

13½"

1½" gap between to fit legs

20"

34½"

Both ends cut at 30 degrees off square, ends are not parallel

5½"

2½"

34½"

20"

2

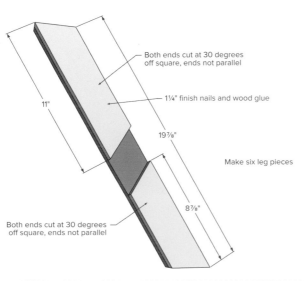

Both ends cut at 30 degrees off square, ends not parallel

1¼" finish nails and wood glue

11"

19⅞"

Make six leg pieces

8⅞"

Both ends cut at 30 degrees off square, ends not parallel

3

1 BENCH SEAT

Drill two ¾" (2cm) pocket holes on each end of all bench-seat boards. Apply glue to ends and attach to breadboard ends, spaced ¼" (6mm) apart, with 1¼" (3cm) pocket hole screws.

2 BENCH-SEAT SUPPORTS

Mark the underside of the bench seat for location of all supports. Drill pilot holes for 2" (5cm) screws and attach the supports to the underside of the bench seat with 2" (5cm) screws and wood glue. Make sure you attach the supports parallel to the breadboard ends by marking with a square.

3 LEGS

Build all six legs by laying all of the full leg pieces out, parallel to one another, with top and bottom angles matching. Lay the smaller leg pieces on top, matching the outside edges. Apply glue on back side of all leg filler pieces and nail down with 1¼" (3cm) finish nails.

4 LEG ASSEMBLY

Pair two leg pieces to create a leg base. Apply glue at the intersection and secure each base with four 1¼" (3cm) finish nails.

5 ATTACHING LEGS

Drill pilot holes for 2¾" wood screws on the legs. Fit the legs between the supports and attach them using wood glue and 2¾" (7cm) screws.

6 ANGLE BRACES

Drill two ¾" (2cm) pocket holes in each end of all angle braces. Attach the angle braces to the legs and the underside of the bench using wood glue and 1¼" (3cm) pocket hole screws.

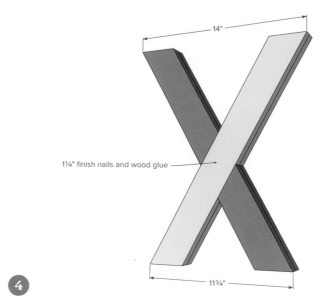

14"

1¼" finish nails and wood glue

11¾"

4

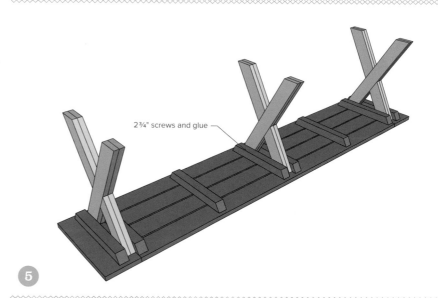

2¾" screws and glue

5

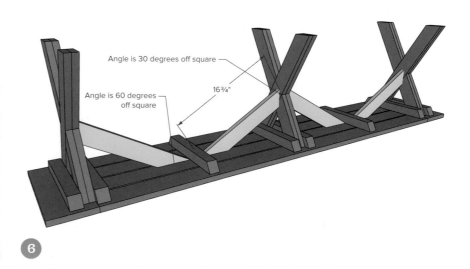

Angle is 30 degrees off square

Angle is 60 degrees off square

16¾"

6

GLOSSARY

APRON Aprons are the upper sides of a table. They are used to support a tabletop and add extra strength to the center of a tabletop.

BARK SIDE Inspect the end grain of a board; the side the grain curves away from is the bark side. When laying multiple boards down for a tabletop, it is important to rotate bark side up, bark side down, bark side up and so on. You do this so that in case the tabletop expands, it will not warp to one side.

BEVEL A bevel differs from a traditional angle cut because the cut stays at square; it is the angle of the cut that changes. For a stool with angled legs, the top and bottom cuts of the legs might be beveled.

BREADBOARD ENDS Used on tabletops to cover end grains of tabletop boards. Normally they are the width of the table and are attached to all tabletop-board ends.

BUILD THE BOX This is a term I use quite a bit. As we build furniture, especially storage furniture, we often simply build a box to begin with. The *box* refers to the basic storage shape of the project.

COUNTERSINK BIT A special drill bit that both predrills and drills an indentation for the screw head at the same time. The countersink bit helps to hide screw heads below the surface of the wood, enabling you to fill the hole with wood filler. Exposed screw heads pose a challenge when finishing and will tear your sandpaper when sanding.

CROSSCUT Cutting across the grain. Most cuts in the cutting lists are simple crosscuts.

DOUBLE BEVEL A double bevel refers to a cut made at an angle off square and beveled at the same time. You will need a compound miter saw to cut double bevels with accuracy.

DRAWER BOX These are the boards that make up the drawer storage area. Sometimes the front side of the drawer box is the drawer face.

DRAWER FACE I like to add drawer faces to drawer boxes because it gives me the opportunity to place a perfect-looking piece to hide any ill-fitting drawer box.

DRY-FIT Testing fit of boards before joining.

EDGE The edge of a board is the narrowest side of the board, running with the grain.

EDGE BANDING Edge banding is veneer sold in ¾"- (2cm-) thick strips, designed to cover exposed plywood edges.

END GRAIN The end grain refers to the end of the wood, cut against the grain.

FACE The face of a board is the widest side of the board, running with the grain.

FACE FRAME Face frames are used to frame the face out of a box. Often face frames are extended into legs, used as lateral support for the box, or used to cover exposed plywood edges.

FASTEN To fasten means to attach one board to another.

FENCE A fence on a saw is the guide that helps you hold your board square when making cuts. Some fences are adjustable; others are fixed.

FLUSH In this book, you will hear the term *flush* often. It means to join the boards so that the two noted edges match up. For example, *flush to the back* would mean the tabletop meets but does not exceed the back of the project.

GRAIN All real-wood products have a grain. This is the direction the tree grows in. It is important to pay attention to grains so that your project looks neat and professional. Always sand and paint with the grain for best results.

GRIT Sandpaper is sold in grits, with lower grits being coarser, and higher grits being finer.

INSET This means to place a door or other piece inside the project. *Inset* can also mean attaching a board to a project set in, and not flush.

MITER Notice how a picture-frame corner is fitted at a 45-degree angle? Or how crown molding is angled to meet in corners? This is *mitering*, and it means you cut both pieces at a 45-degree angle to form a 90-degree corner.

MOLDING Molding is store-bought wood with decorative patterns. Plans can use molding in a variety of ways to add character and interest to a project.

OVERHANG (OR OVEREXTEND) The distance a board hangs over the project.

PREDRILL This is accomplished by drilling a small pilot hole in the wood before driving a screw. Pilot holes (page 28) should be drilled to the depth of the screw to prevent wood-splitting.

RIP Meaning to cut boards lengthwise, with the grain, this is most often used to change the width of a board or convert sheet goods into board widths. Ripping is done with a table saw or circular saw.

SPLIT When a screw or nail is driven into wood, sometimes the wood will separate or split. You can avoid splitting by predrilling screw holes. Wood is more likely to split near cuts, knots, or existing cracks, so use caution when fastening in these known problem areas.

SQUARE To be square means your corners are all right angles or 90 degrees. *Checking for square* means measuring from opposite corners at a diagonal and matching up the two opposing measurements.

SUPPORT This is a board that's purely supportive. Usually, these boards are not visible in the finished project.

TRIM These are any boards added to the box or, most commonly, smaller wood boards that can be both decorative and supportive.

VENEER This is a thin layer of wood that is most likely laminated and added over less-desirable wood species on sheet goods.

ACKNOWLEDGMENTS

Just a few years ago, I was a simple housewife living in remote Alaska, with a dream. A dream so far-fetched, I was afraid to share it even with my own family.

There were too many diapers to change, dinners to cook, and miles for me to even imagine that I might get my ideas about building furniture into a book.

Not knowing where to start, and without any professional experience or formal education, I turned to strangers and poured out my furniture plans free to the public on my blog. And you embraced me, you believed in me. You gave me the confidence and experience I needed to follow my dreams.

This book is dedicated to you. To each and every person who has ever visited my blog. Your comments, your projects, your e-mails, and your support have helped me get here. I cannot thank you enough.

It is almost selfish for a mother to have a dream of her own. To be able to follow her own aspirations and seek more from life than the children she is proud of. Mothers by nature are selfless, giving vessels, not ever asking for more fulfillment than a healthy, happy family.

Yet my family saw my needs and found a way to support me as I chased a crazy dream that had no sure-success ending. This book is for my husband, Jacob, and my daughter Grace, who ate hundreds of burnt dinners and sacrificed so much to give me a chance to follow my dreams.

For my mother, who taught me that you can make anything from nothing, and that your children are the most important DIY projects of all. For my sisters and brothers, nieces and nephews, and especially, my husband's family, who has welcomed me as their own, and supported me through it all. You stepped up to help, and I am very thankful and know this book would not have been possible without your help.

And with special thanks, I thank each and every contributor to this book. You have inspired me and challenged me to become better. You have become my friends, and I am so honored that you said yes. Thank you for putting in the extra time and effort. Thank you for being amazing.

And a final thank-you to those who work tirelessly behind the scenes, but are so important to the success of this book. To John, my manager, and his wife, Amanda. To my agent, Devin, and my editor, Betty.

And to all the hands involved in putting this book into your hands—thank you.

RESOURCES

The majority of the materials and tools used in this book can be purchased at your local home improvement store or chain.

HOME IMPROVEMENT STORES

Lowes **lowes.com**

The Home Depot **homedepot.com**

Menards **menards.com**

Ace Hardware **acehardware.com**

True Value **truevalue.com**

SPECIALTY STORES AND PRODUCTS

Kreg Tool Company
kregtool.com
Manufacturers of the pocket hole jig.

Osbourne Wood
osbournewood.net
Manufacturers of the turned legs on kitchen island project.

Rockler Woodworking
rockler.com
Hard-to-find hardware

Columbia Forest Products
columbiaforestproducts.com/purebond
PureBond formaldehyde-free plywood.

CONTRIBUTOR BIOS

AMANDA CLARK is an Iowa farmgirl turned Colorado pharmacist. She loves spending time with her husband, building furniture, photographing anything and everything, and enjoying all that life has to offer. She built her first Ana White–designed bench in 2010 and hasn't stopped building since.

AMANDA CRAWFORD (amandacrawfordphotography.com) finds her happiness in making things with her hands and sharing them with others. She is married to John and has three wonderful children, Jacey, Lucas, and Jocelyn, who inspire most everything that she does.

JAIME COSTIGLIO (www.thatsmyletter. blogspot.com) is married with three children. She enjoys making and changing things by building, painting, and sewing.

HILLARY DICKMAN (www.thefriendlyhome .blogspot.com) is the mother of two girls. She grew up in Lafayette, California, and graduated from Miami University in Oxford, Ohio, with a master's degree in speech communication. In addition to building furniture, her time is currently consumed by creating a school and community garden for her neighborhood elementary school.

KRISTEN DUKE (www.kristenduke photography.com) is a lifestyle photographer in Austin, Texas. She is the mother of four energetic children and married to the man of her dreams. She teaches camera workshops and is the author of *Say No to Auto,* a photography book on learning the basics of a 'big fancy" camera

CHERISH FIELDER is a stay-at-home mom who loves photography, cooking, and painting everything in sight!

WHITNEY GAINER (www.shanty-2-chic. com) is a stay-at-home mom to five kids. She has attempted most every craft, finding that she loves the process of creating her own treasures. She is often found with paint, old furniture, her sewing machine, and tools.

AMY HUNTLEY (www.theidearoom.net) is the owner and author of *The Idea Room.* She is the mother of five, who enjoys sharing her love of all things creative in the hopes of inspiring other women and families.

LYDIA MANDERS lives in southwest Colorado. She is an awesome wife and mother of Westie Sally and labradoodle Donnelly. Outside of her full-time career, Lydia enjoys the outdoors, sunshine, Jeeps, being on the lake, and learning new skills.

ASHLEY MILLS (www.thehandmadehome. net) is a southern gal and mommy of three who constantly wears paint stains on her clothes. She is a writer who shares the fun of motherhood, an artist who rarely takes herself too seriously, and a designer who loves the graphic appeal of simple elements.

LAYLA PALMER (www.theletteredcottage. com) lives in the deep South (Prattville, Alabama, to be exact). Her blog is nicknamed "The Lettered Cottage" because of a passion for writing and a love of older homes.

REBECCA RIDNER (BeccaDaleDesigns. com) makes her home in the hills of east Tennessee and can be identified by her well-loved cowboy boots, paint-splattered hair, and power tool in hand. She has four young kids and a practical husband who complements her creative personality perfectly.

CRYSTAL ROSE (Thereadinggirl.com) often spent idle school days rearranging furniture and redecorating rooms in her parent's home as a young girl. While she ultimately went on to become an attorney, after finding herself a newlywed in a sparsely decorated home, she discovered her first carpentry cravings.

ASHLEY TURNER (www.shanty-2-chic. com) is a wife, mother of three, and passionate DIY-er. Ashley started building furniture two years ago and has nearly furnished her entire house with her bare hands.

SHAUNNA AND MATT WEST (www. perfectlyimperfectblog.com) live in Troy, Alabama. Shaunna shares her stories on DIY projects, furniture makeovers, and family adventures on the Perfectly Imperfect blog, and has been featured on *The Nate Berkus Show, Cottages & Bungalows*, Design*Sponge, and Apartment Therapy.

BROOK WILHELMSEN is a military spouse who has moved eleven times in the last fourteen years. No matter where she lives, her goal is to "Create Awesome."

KIRSTEN WRIGHT (www.thecraftingchicks. com) is the mother of three little boys and one little girl. Her professional photography skills, her eye for design, and the creative projects she has showcased on thecraftingchicks.com have led to many television appearances and features on popular websites like Apartment Therapy's Ohdeedoh, Martha Stewart, and many more.

INDEX